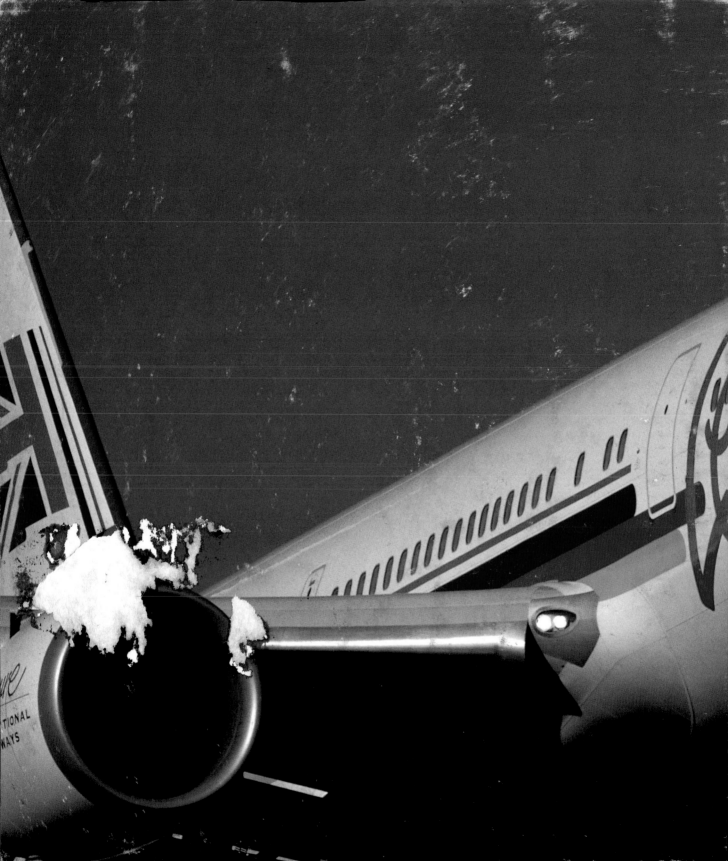

BOEING JETLINERS

Guy Norris & Mark Wagner

BARNES
&NOBLE
BOOKS
NEW YORK

This edition published by Barnes & Noble, Inc.,
by arrangement with Motorbooks International
Publishers

1998 Barnes & Noble Books

M 10 9 8 7 6 5 4 3 2 1

ISBN 0-7607-0900-9

First published in 1996 by Motorbooks International
Publishers & Wholesalers

Library of Congress Cataloging-in-Publication Data
Available

On the front cover: The 747-121 *Clipper Juan Trippe*
is named after the chairman of Pan Am, Juan Trippe.
Trippe was intrumental in Pan Am's decision to place
the launch order for the 747 and introduce it to
passenger service.

On the frontispiece: A Southern Air Transport 747-
200 displays a few of the large dimensions of its
fuselage.

On the title page: Here one of Air UK Leisure's 767-
300s displays the wing's track-mounted leading edge
slats and double-slotted inboard trailing flaps as it
lands at London Gatwick.

On the back cover: The 747 is truly a world-
shrinker. No version, nor operator, is a better
reflection of this than the 747-438s flown by
Australian national airline, Qantas.

Printed in Hong Kong

Contents

Acknowledgments

Thanks to all of the Boeing staff, particularly Brian Ames, Tom Cole, Susan Davis, John Dern, Kirsti Dunn, Mark Hooper, Donna Mikov, Stephanie Mudgett, Barbara Murphy, Steve Smith, Steve Thieme, and Chris Villiers. Additional thanks for propulsion research to Rick Kennedy of General Electric and Robert Nuttall of Rolls-Royce. Appreciation for early research help to Jonathan Bregazzi, Mark Byrne, Nick Cook, Rob Grundy, Mark Thorpe, and Stephen J. White. For photographic help thanks to Fauzi Ahmad, John Bailey, John Braden, Art Carson, Bruce Drum, Dennis Fernandez, Kimberly Foster, Ruth Golden, Eddie Ha, Andy Marsh, Bruce May, Schnozz Meyer, Jim Reynolds, Pat Schoneberger, Sergey Sergeyev, Edwin Shum, Resham Singh, Hernando Vergara, Rudi Voller, Anna Walker, Tom Winfrey, Wilai and Kai (Thai), Joseph Yung, and Yuzer Yusoff. Thanks to Jan, John, and Larry for support and to Judy, Tom, Greg, and Lucy Bristow for endless patience. Our gratitude also to Allan Winn of Flight International, and Michael Haenggi of Motorbooks International.

Guy Norris is the Los Angeles-based West Coast Editor of *Flight International* magazine.

Mark Wagner is *Flight International*'s London-based photographer and a licensed pilot.

Introduction

March 1, 1996 was a special day for Boeing and the air transport industry it serves. The 8,000th Boeing commercial jetliner, a 767-300ER in the colors of KLM Royal Dutch Airlines, was handed over to the International Lease Finance Corporation (ILFC).

The achievement marked a major milestone for Boeing. By 1996 the Seattle-based company had delivered 54 percent of the 14,700 jetliners produced by the world's commercial manufacturers since the dawn of the civil jet age in 1952. More than 16.3 billion passengers had flown on its jetliners on journeys that would be equal to flying to the sun and back 700 times.

Although the event was a recognition of the continuing popularity of Boeing's individual models, the handover was also a testament to the success of its "family of airliners" approach. This vital ingredient may well have emerged by serendipity rather than design but it has been at the heart of the company's strategy for years.

Competition is fierce however, and getting stronger, so Boeing is not resting on its laurels. To maintain its lead, Boeing is expanding its family in every sector from 100 seats to 600 seats. The New Generation 737 family is set for entry into service in the late 1990s and will be joined by new derivatives of the 757 and possibly the 767. The 777 program, heralded by much of the industry as a benchmark for the 21st century, will fulfill the re-equipment needs of airlines for an unprecedented number of roles. The 747, long established in a league of its own, will almost certainly be stretched and re-winged to maintain Boeing's dominance at the high capacity end of the market.

This book details the growth of this remarkable family and provides an insight into the design philosophy that forged each member. It also reveals some of the key reasons for the popularity of Boeing jetliners and looks at some coming developments.

Guy Norris
Newport Beach, California

CHAPTER ONE

707

First of the Many

In the history of commercial enterprise, there can be few gambles that have paid as handsomely as Boeing's 1952 $16 million decision to go ahead with development of a prototype jet airliner. Three years later, Pan American World Airways ordered the new aircraft, dubbed the 707, launching Boeing into a 44-year global domination of the commercial jetliner business.

The origins of this famous airliner can be traced to 1949 and 1950, when Boeing began outline studies of a jet transport design called the 473-60C. Although not greatly detailed, it was a four-engined swept-wing concept. Boeing's new B-47 and B-52 bombers made it the undisputed champion of big swept-wing designs, and it seemed natural to transfer this to the civil market. Although no airline seemed to be interested at the time, the promise of jet-powered transports was undeniable and studies continued.

One of the most historically significant airframes in commercial aviation, the weary 707 prototype, Dash 80 is pictured on the ramp at Boeing Field, 41 years to the month after its first flight in July 1954. Rescued from obscurity in the vast desert boneyard of Davis Monthan Air Force Base, Arizona, Dash 80 was flown back to Seattle by Boeing on behalf of its owner, the Smithsonian Institution.

Jet-powered derivatives of the Model 367 Stratocruiser, or C-97 as it was designated by the U. S. Air Force, were also underway. The big propeller aircraft, itself based on the B-29 Superfortress, was already giving clues that the future was in jets. The USAF complained that its new Boeing-built B-47 jet bombers were almost stalling in their efforts to refuel from the slow flying C-97.

The biggest clues of all, however, came from overseas. The British were hard at work developing the de Havilland D.H.106 Comet and had already flown this graceful jet airliner in July 1949. Only two weeks later, Avro Canada flew the ambitious C.102 Jetliner. Close behind came the Russians, who were studying passenger-carrying vari-

ants of the Tupolev Tu-16 Badger bomber, later to become known as the Tu-104.

Spurred by the signs around it, Boeing focused on a design that could provide the basis for a tanker/transport in military guise and for a 100-seater airliner in a commercial role. The company chose the opportunity to launch the 700-series of products, the -500 being reserved for gas turbines and the -600 for missiles. By all rights, the new aircraft should have been named the Boeing 700; but possibly for superstitious reasons and because it sounded better, it was designated 707. Seven is a sacred or mystic number, composed of four and three, which from time immemorial have been accounted lucky numbers.

Distinguished by its short fuselage, this early model 707 is seen during the twilight of its career at Zurich Airport, Switzerland, in October 1988. This aircraft first flew in January 1959 and was the 10th production 707 off the line. Just over two years into service, American Airlines opted to convert it to the more efficient -123B turbofan configuration at the then considerable cost of around $1 million. The airline got its money's worth by operating it for 20 years before selling it to Cyprus Airways.

The first public use of the model number 707 was still a long way off, however, and the prototype carried the model number 367-80. This was both a thinly veiled disguise to confuse the competition and a recognition of the connection with the early C-97 (or Model 367) derivative studies.

The "Dash-80," as it later became widely known, could not have looked more different from the C-97. It followed the B-47 and B-52 in having a swept-back wing to allow cruise at high Mach number and four jet engines mounted in pods well forward and below the wing. Early Dash-80 designs carried two jets in a single pod under each wing, but this was later rejected in favor of separate pods for each engine.

The wing swept up at 7 degrees and back at 35 degrees from thick roots which carried the two-spar fail-safe structure through the body in one continuous center-section. The fuselage was a "double-bubble" cross section formed by two interconnecting arcs of different radii. The larger radii formed the roof section and was faired into the lower arc to form a smooth ellipse. The undercarriage was made up of two main four-wheel trucks, which retracted inward to the centerline of the fuselage to occupy large gear bays and a two-wheel nose gear assembly.

The Dash-80 emerged from Boeing's Renton facility in May 1954 and would probably have flown in late June if it were not for the unexpected failure during fast taxi trials of the left main

Having spent the first four years of its career with Continental, this -324C moved on to serve with Brazilian flag-carrier Varig, in 1972. The C model retained its value longer than many of its earlier sister aircraft because it *had a strengthened floor and stronger undercarriage to take heavy cargo loads. It is pictured approaching London Gatwick airport in October 1993 wearing the livery of Angolan Air Charter.*

landing gear. Unfortunately, this punched a jagged hole straight through the wing. After the gear was strengthened, the Dash-80 finally launched Boeing into a new era with its first flight on July 15, 1954.

As Boeing hoped, military interest in the Dash-80 matured the same month into an order for 29 tanker versions from the USAF. Produced under the Boeing model number of 717, the aircraft is better known as the KC-135. Superficially identical to the Dash-80, the KC-135 differs mainly in having a single large cargo door and an unobstructed upper deck floor for cargo and troops. In all, Boeing built more than 800 tankers and other special purpose versions before production ended in 1966.

In July 1955, the USAF gave formal approval for Boeing to sign up commercial operators of the aircraft. First up off the mark was Pan Am, which ordered 20 with the designation 707-120. The airline had originally ordered three de Havilland Comets but cancelled them in 1954 when the British airliner was grounded after two mysterious crashes. The cause turned out to be fatigue which at the time was a little understood phenomenon. Comets were beefed-up and redesigned, but it was a case of too-little, too-late, and the initiative was lost forever to the United States.

To the industry's surprise, Pan Am simultaneously ordered 25 Douglas DC-8s. This was to be the arch-rival of the 707 but had not even flown by this stage! Boeing was getting worried because Douglas was signing up orders for DC-8s from its loyal airlines like Delta, United, and Eastern. Douglas was turning the late development of the DC-8 to its

A rare survivor of the long-range, short fuselage -138 series developed specially for the trans-Pacific routes of Qantas, the Australian national airline. Qantas took delivery of this aircraft as VH-EBM in September 1964. It later passed through the hands of Braniff and Boeing before operating for TAG Aviation. The turbofan-powered 138B was basically the same as the original -120 series but was 10 feet (3.1 m) shorter. Note the ventral fin.

12

advantage by designing its "paper" aircraft to be bigger, more powerful, and longer-ranged.

In near desperation, Boeing went to American Airlines. American complained that the fuselage of the 707 was too narrow compared to the DC-8, which could seat six-abreast. The manufacturer was in a tight spot. The fuselage of the 707 was supposed to be the same as the KC-135 for which Boeing expected large orders. Making them different would destroy any commonality between the production lines. In the end, Boeing decided to "bite-the-bullet" and widened the fuselage by 16 inches (41 cm) to 12 feet 4 inches (3.76 m), making it about 1 inch (2.5 cm) larger than the DC-8.

The brave decision probably saved the civil 707 project and, in doing so, indirectly ensured the destiny of the 707's commercial successors. It certainly satisfied American, which ordered 32. Other major changes were afoot, including a larger wing to hold more fuel for intercontinental ranges, a longer fuselage to seat more passengers, and more powerful engines to get the whole thing off the ground. A directional stability problem encountered during early test flights also meant a slightly larger tail fin. All these

This former TWA 707-331B survived a 1969 bomb attack in Damascus to fly for another 11 years with the airline before being stored and withdrawn from use at Kansas City. The aircraft, which was fitted with a completely new nose section after the blast, was eventually flown to Davis Monthan Air Force Base, Arizona, where tails and engines were removed for use on USAF KC-135E tankers.

Early model 707s used water-injection to boost takeoff power and were nicknamed "aqua-jets" and "water-wagons" by their crews. The method is still used by non re-engined KC-135 tankers and the dramatic effect is well illustrated in this morning takeoff from Edwards AFB, California, in February 1994.

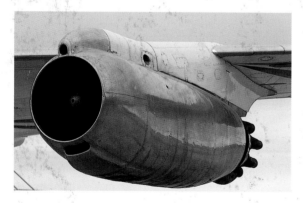

This rare contemporary view of a Pratt & Whitney JT4A engine on the wing of a 707 was captured in the Mojave Desert where, ironically, General Electric used this aircraft, N707GE, as a testbed for the very latest CFM56 engine series. This 707 was originally delivered to Pan Am as Clipper Bald Eagle in April 1960. P&W supplied this more powerful engine to Douglas for the DC-8 and later to Boeing.

changes added to the cost of the program, which took eight years to break even.

Turbojet Thunder

The first production version, the -120, flew first in 1957 and could seat up to 181 passengers. Despite achieving revolutionary speeds, it was essentially underpowered. Its Pratt & Whitney JT3C-6 turbojets were incredibly noisy and dirty. They were rated at only 13,500 pounds of thrust each and needed water injection for takeoff at high weights. This process involved the injection of distilled water into the compressor, which basically fooled the engine into believing it was sucking in more air than it actually was. This boosted power, but was environmentally disasterous and took up valuable weight that would have otherwise been used for payload or fuel.

Interim versions were produced that were almost tailor-made to individual airline requirements. A -138 version with a 10-foot shorter fuselage than the -120 was bought by Qantas of Australia for long range trans-Pacific routes. Another was the -220, powered by 15,800-pound thrust JT4A-3s and bought by Braniff for services to high-altitude airports in South America.

The big change, however, was the -320 Intercontinental which was first introduced on the 16th production 707 in January 1959. Wing span was increased by more than 11 feet to 142 feet 5 inches, producing a 2.5 percent aerodynamic improvement over the original wing, while the fuselage was stretched by almost 8 feet to 152 feet 11 inches.

Boeing never looked back from the decision to go for the -320, which was driven mainly by competition from the DC-8. By late 1957, the 707 order book took on a decidedly healthier look with 145 orders, compared with 124 for the DC-8. The Douglas jet never caught up, and its production ended with 556 sold, compared with the 1,010 commercial and military variants of the 707 and 720. The last commercial 707, a -320C was sold to the Moroccan government in March 1982.

Military versions continued to be produced until 1991 when the last 707 airframe was delivered to the UK Royal Air Force as an E-3D radar-

Pratt & Whitney's JT3D turbofan revolutionized the performance of the 707 and its contemporaries. It was developed
from the JT3C turbojet to meet the challenge of the Rolls-Royce

Conway and ultimately led to standardization on the -320B
and -320C models. The intake on top of the engine admits air
to turbocompressors that provide pressurized air to the cabin.

equipped airborne early warning (AEW) aircraft. In an ironic twist of fate, the RAF selected the E-3D, (as the UK's versions were designated) over the AEW Nimrod, a military version of the ill-fated Comet.

Increased engine power was the key to the -320's success. The first "Intercontinentals" were equipped with the 15,800-pound thrust JT4A-3, or -5 engines, and later -9s, but the big difference came when the first turbofans were developed.

Enter the Turbofans

The use of turbofans was a turning point in commercial jet history. Turbofans generate a lot of their thrust by passing large volumes of air quickly through a fan at the front of the engine. This air "bypasses" the core of the engine, which produces the power necessary to turn the front fan. The fan air not only adds thrust to the engine but shrouds the hot and noisy stream coming from the center of the jet to help quiet the exhaust noise. The more air that passes through the engine without being used for combustion, the higher the bypass ratio.

The first commercial high-bypass ratio turbofan was the 17,500-pound thrust Rolls-Royce Conway Mk 508. This equipped the 707-420 that was ordered by El Al and British Overseas Airways Corporation (known as BOAC, later to be merged with British European Airways and become British Airways).

Engine controls, gauges, and a weather radar display dominate this view of a classic "steam cockpit" in this -323B. The term "steam" denotes the use of basic electromechani- *cal, analogue instrument technology, which is relatively unchanged since World War II. Modern flight decks are less cluttered and use TV-like, or "glass cockpit," displays.*

U. S. forces have the world's largest fleet of military 707 derivatives. The vast majority are KC-135 air-to-air refueling tankers as seen in this line-up. However, many are used for special missions such as the WC-135B weather observation aircraft in the foreground. Note the refueling boom stowed beneath the tail, allowing it to be quickly converted back for tanking. In all, Boeing built 88 special-use variants for the USAF, the last of which was delivered in 1966.

The type entered service in 1960. The first aircraft destined for BOAC were fitted with an additional fin located below the tail to comply with British airworthiness regulations for additional lateral stability. These requirements were eased for later 707s on the British register. Spurred by the development of the Conway, Pratt & Whitney produced the more efficient JT3D-3 engine, which generated up to 18,000 pounds of thrust. This transformed the 707-320 family, leading to production of the -320B, which could carry 189 passengers up to 6,000 miles. The powerful, yet more fuel-efficient engines were also fitted with complex double-thrust reversers that, when used in combination with the new leading and trailing edge flaps, dramatically improved landing performance. In addition, cruise performance was boosted by the development of low drag streamwise wing tips.

A cargo, or mixed cargo-passenger version of the -320B, called the -320C Convertible, was also developed. As a freighter, its large 91-inch-by-134-inch (2.3-m by 3.4-m) forward cargo door could swallow 96,126 pounds (43,600 kg) of payload or, in passenger form, could seat 202 people if fitted with two extra emergency exits.

Military Use

Just as the newer engines revived the slow commercial sales of the early 707, they also boosted military sales. The 707 was selected for the presidential fleet— the most prestigious military role in the United States—and now holds the distinction of being the first jet-powered presidential aircraft. It also broke new ground for Boeing. Until the delivery of the first VC-137 in May 1959, presidential transports had been the preserve of Douglas with the DC-4 and DC-6, and Lockheed with the VC-121E Super Constellation. The role has since stayed in Boeing's hands and today's Air Force One is a military 747-200, designated E-4A.

The large radome of the E-3 AWACS (airborne warning and control system) easily makes it the most recognizable military variant of the 707. The 30 foot (9.1 m) diameter rotordome houses a Westinghouse surveillance radar which rotates up to six times per minute. Earlier JT3D-powered versions like the E-3C pictured above can stay on patrol more than 11 hours without refueling. Later CFM56 versions can fly unrefueled for more than 10 hours but can patrol around 1,000 feet higher at more than 30,000 feet (9,145 m). A total of 68 707-based AWACS were built for the USAF, NATO, Saudi Arabia, France, and the UK.

18

The refueling boom of this tanker, seen extended during this fly-by at RAF Fairford in the UK, is controlled by an operator housed beneath the tail using the two movable fins near the end of the boom. More than half of the 732 tankers built were still in service as late as 1995, some 30 years after the last one rolled off the production line. The tankers have been re-engined and strengthened with new wing skins to extend their lives beyond the year 2020. Some have been re-engined with ex-airline PW JT3D-3B turbofans, though more than 400 KC-135Rs have also been fitted with the more efficient CFM56. The new engine is expected to save the USAF around $1.7 billion in fuel bills over 15 years or, to put it another way, enough to fill up 7.7 million U. S. cars every year for a decade and a half.

Some old airliners have taken on a new lease of life as special role military 707s. This E-6A/YE-8B airframe represents two new versions. The CFM56-powered E-6A TACAMO (Take Charge And Move Out) used by the U. S. Navy to contact missile-equipped submarines in time of war, and the E-8 JSTARS (Joint Surveillance and Target Attack Radar System). JSTARS can pick out individual tanks more than 100 miles (160 km) behind enemy lines and was used successfully by the USAF and Army during the 1991 Gulf War. The wingtip pods on an E-6A contain a threat warning ALR-66 electronic support measures system and aerials to receive satellite communications. The long aerial beneath the pod is for standard HF (high frequency) radio communications. Maximum E-6A unrefueled endurance is 16.2 hours, while additional refueling in mid-air can extend this to 72 hours.

The additional range and payload of the -320B made the aircraft an ideal platform for other military uses. In the latter stages of its production life, many 707s were turned out to the U. S. Air Force as E-3A AEW Sentrys (commonly known as AWACS), sporting distinctive radar dishes on pylons above the rear fuselage. Foreign sales of the E-3 amounted to 68 aircraft. Some of the last 707 airframes made, by now powered by the General Electric/Snecma CFM56-2A turbofans, were E-6A TACAMO long-range communications aircraft for the U. S. Navy.

True Strength

Of all the Boeing 700-series products, the 707 has amassed the largest number of stories which attest to its rugged strength and extraordinary survivability. During its first decade of service, two incredible incidents occured that demonstrated this toughness. In June 1968, a heavily laden Pan Am 707 left San Francisco International for Honolulu. During the flight, the No. 1 engine exploded, ripping away 25 feet of the right wing along with the nacelle and pylon. The crew managed to nurse the damaged airliner across the bay to a naval air station for a successful emergency landing.

In December of that same year, a TWA 707 collided in mid-air over New York with an Eastern Lockheed Constellation. The 707 lost 35 feet from its left wing, but miraculously managed to land at John F. Kennedy International Airport. The "Connie" was not so lucky.

Another Pan Am 707-120, in the dawn of its career, was mid-Atlantic at 35,000 feet en-route to New York from Paris when it slipped out of trim and nosed over into a dive. As it hurtled toward the ocean, the jet almost reached the speed of sound reaching Mach 0.95 before being hauled straight and level by the crew at only 6,000 feet. Investigators believe the airframe was subjected to loads of up to 5 Gs, compared to the structural design limit of 3.75 Gs.

The incident damaged the horizontal stabilizers, ailerons, and some wing panels, but left the 707 otherwise intact. The Pam Am aircraft remained in

A LAN Chile-owned 707-385C rounds-out for touchdown at just over 130 mph on a warm Los Angeles day. Most of the civilian 707s now left in service are

dedicated cargo aircraft, though this particular aircraft was later bought by the Chilean Air Force after this scene was captured.

service for many years afterwards with its wings permanently bent upwards by 2 inches (5 cm)!

More recently, a chartered 707-321C freighter was climbing over the Swiss Alps at 36,000 feet (11,000 m) en-route from Luxembourg to Africa in March 1992, when both starboard engines sheared off the wing, complete with their pylons. With a serious fire in the wing and no flaps, the pilot and crew remarkably landed the crippled jet at Istres Air Base in France. The pilot used full left controls and differential power on his remaining two engines to land at the very high speed of 190 knots (350 km/h) with a 25 knot tailwind.

This and a similar incident involving a KC-135 during the Gulf War are thought to be the only known occasions when a four-engined jet airliner has had two engines separate from the same wing and still managed to land safely. Both missing engines from the freighter were later found within one half mile of each other in a Swiss mountain top forest.

No, not a novel five-engined Boeing. This 720 once plied the sky for TWA, Northwest Orient, Maersk Air, Nigeria Airways, Trans European, and Conair, but now finds use as AlliedSignal's engine testbed based at Phoenix Sky Harbor airport in Arizona. The 720 is pictured here with a new variant of the TFE731 business jet engine mounted on the test strut.

Another view of AlliedSignal's 720-051B testbed. The shorter-bodied 720 was originally designed for short to medium routes and was at first going to be called the 717. This designation was later given to the military tanker version which became known as the

KC-135. The aircraft was then redesignated the 707-020 before reverting to the 720, the only Boeing commercial not to end in the number seven. Production ended after 154 were made as the 727 took over the market.

CHAPTER TWO

727

Boeing's Trijet

With its large T-tail, clean wing, and clustered engines, the 727 is totally unlike any other civil or military aircraft ever produced by Boeing. Even by today's standards the highly swept wings give the jet a sleeker look than many of its more modern successors. Above all, its durability and dependability have kept the 727 in the "front-line" of airline operations right up to the mid-1990s and more than 1,000 examples remain active in all parts of the world. By 1993, this included the Confederation of Independent States (former Soviet Union), representing the massive market penetration that has been forged by this well-liked airliner.

The 727 has an important place in Boeing's history because it represents the beginning of the company's hugely successful "family" approach to the airline. Since it was designed to fill a smaller, yet more diverse market sector than the 707, it was built to fly from diverse airports across short-, medium-, or long-range routes. As a result, Boeing ended up with what is arguably the world's first truly versatile jet airliner. It could shuttle along busy air corridors between major cities or lift large

Storm clouds gather over the Persian Gulf as an Emirates Airlines 727-200 powers out of Dubai on a hot 90 degree winter afternoon.

passenger loads from small runways. It would boldly go where no jet airliner had gone before, and open up a potentially huge new market.

At least this is what the planners hoped in 1960 when they started offering the 727 to airlines. The traditionally conservative Boeing board, still smarting from the recent and painful losses of jet bomber and fighter contracts and laboring under a sluggish 707 market, was not convinced that the 727 would be a success and worried about the estimated $150 million development tag carried by the program. Yet project studies started as far back as 1956 convinced some Boeing board members that it needed a short- to medium-range stablemate for the 707. The public's rapidly growing love affair with jets

meant a big replacement market for the smaller piston airliners. Even in the late 1950s and early 1960s, fleets of World War II technology propeller-driven aircraft like the Douglas DC-4, DC-6, the later derivative DC-7, and Lockheed Constellations still growled slowly around the world. Newer turboprops such as the Lockheed Electra and Vickers Viscount were selling well, but the airlines were attracted by the speed and capacity of pure jets. Speed meant passengers and passengers meant money.

However, Boeing was not the only jet maker, and its new 727 would have to fight for a market share. It faced the ugly spectre of competition from foreign aircraft makers as well as its old Californian-based adversaries, Douglas and Convair.

Early models of the 727, like this 1965-vintage -100, continue to provide operators with useful midsize freight capacity. This jet spent its first 24 years carrying passengers for launch customer, Eastern Airlines, before the carrier went bankrupt and it passed on to FedEx which converted it into a freighter. The aircraft now has the same large (7 foot 2 inch by 11 foot 2 inch wide) cargo door as the 707-320C and beefed-up floor structure. It can take loads of up to 44,000 pounds (20,000 kg) on short to medium routes but is also able to take a 30,000 pound (13,600 kg) payload up to 2,300 miles (3,700 km).

24

Douglas was busy courting big U. S. airlines like United with a mini-version of the DC-8, and Convair was convinced its CV-880 could be developed to perform economically on distances ranging from 300 nm to 3,000 nm.

Meanwhile in Europe, Sud-Aviation (later part of the French company Aerospatiale) was selling the Caravelle—the first jetliner with tail-mounted engines. However, it seated less than 100 passengers. Boeing also saw competition coming from several British aircraft under study, including the Bristol 200 and Avro 740. Among the British threats, Boeing's biggest concern was the de Havilland DH.121 Trident. Unlike its American counterpart, the Trident was being designed around the specific requirements of one airline, British European Airways (BEA). BEA wanted a jet that could carry around 100 passengers at up to 600 mph over the short- to medium-length routes in its European network. While it was fast, the overall design limits made the Trident too small and limited in range for most of the airlines in the United States.

Even though the Trident was designed specifically for BEA's needs, the 727 did not escape the notice of BEA chairman Lord Douglas. Douglas noted the similarities with the British design, each having three tail-mounted engines and a T-tail. He invited the two companies to talk about a possible merging of the two projects and, accordingly, visits were exchanged. In the end, there was no

This former American Airlines 727-100 first flew in December 1966 and plied the American network as a passenger jet until 1984 when it was converted to a cargo configuration and operated by Flying Tigers. This famous cargo carrier merged with Fedex in 1989. When viewed from the front, the only distinguishing feature of the shorter -100 series trijet from its longer -200 brethren is the oval center (or No. 2) engine intake in the base of the tail.

collaboration and the two aircraft went their different ways. Although the Trident was developed into three different versions, the largest of which seated up to 180, total production amounted to only 117. The 727, in contrast, was made into just two basic versions and a grand total of 1,831 were sold before the last -200 was delivered in September 1984.

Chief Design Features

Boeing wrestled with two major airlines, Eastern and United, during the late 1950s as the design was coming together. Eastern was in favor of two engines as the most economical solution, while United wanted four because it wanted a powerful aircraft capable of operating safely into Denver's high-altitude airport (Denver's runways are 5,000 feet above sea level). Eventually they compromised and opted for three, so Boeing studied putting one in the root of the tail, like the Trident, and one engine under each wing. Other versions that never got further than the drawing board had two engines at the tail and a third on top of one of the wings!

Finally, the familiar tail-mounted trijet design was adopted; as this would give a low cabin noise level, an uncluttered wing with better short take-off and landing capability, and better control in case of an engine failure. The team then looked at the fuselage and decided to adopt the same basic cross section as the 707. This would give six abreast seating which, with a length of 133 feet, would give enough seating room for 131. Market predictions, and above all the lower seating capacity (only 110) of the competing Convair CV-880, showed that this was the right decision.

The other key factor about the 727 was the extraordinarily advanced high-lift system which

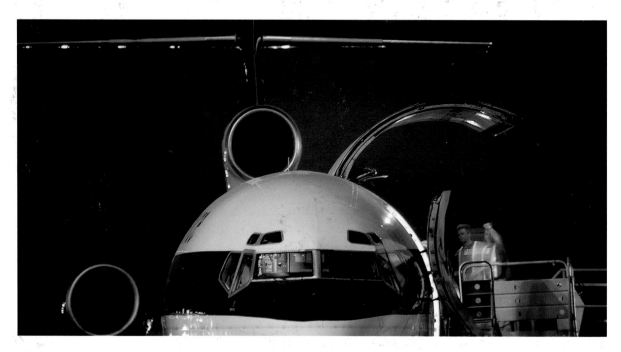

Although this old 727 has been flying since July 1968, it has now been re-engined and could easily be flying to 2020 or beyond. In May 1990, United Parcel Service (UPS) decided to replace all the original PW JT8D engines on its 727-100 fleet with the Rolls-Royce Tay 651-54. The resulting aircraft is distinguished by the much-larger intakes needed for the higher bypass engine (which easily meets the Stage 3 noise rules that come into effect at the end of the 1990s). Most other operators have decided to opt for the less costly option of hush-kitting their 727s as a short-to-medium-term solution.

was designed for the wing. This was crucial to getting the aircraft into and out of smaller airports. It was an essential element in meeting Eastern's requirements to fly from the shortest runway at New York's La Guardia Airport to Miami with a full load. The resulting airfoil had Krueger flaps packed inboard, a long slat along the outboard leading edge, and sophisticated triple-slotted flaps along the trailing edge. When it was all hanging out, the 1,700 square foot wing area suddenly increased by 25 percent and enabled the jet to take off and land at lower speeds. When it was tucked away for high-speed cruise, the slim, swept-back wing gave a maximum cruising speed of 605 mph, outpacing even a few military aircraft at that time.

The 727 also had a few novelties tucked away beneath its skin. The aircraft was the first Boeing jetliner to have hydraulically powered flight controls and, as part of its plan to go to primitive airfields where jets did not usually venture, it also carried its own little powerplant to make it independent of ground power units. The 727 therefore

Pictured on climbout from London Heathrow en-route to Berlin, Germany, this Pan American 727-235 was one of the earliest -200s in service when it was originally delivered to National Airlines in April 1968. The sophisticated high-lift devices are clearly seen on the wing in this view, particularly the four leading-edge slats on the outer section, and the three Krueger leading-edge flaps on the inboard section of each wing.

became the first jet airliner to have the now familiar auxiliary power unit.

The 727 was originally designed around an Allison-built version of the Rolls-Royce Spey. However, this was rejected by Eastern Airlines, and Boeing went instead to Pratt & Whitney for a solution. The resulting JT8D engine was derived from a military turbojet and has gone on to be the most popular jet engine in history with more than 14,000 built!

Family Tree

The first 727, designated E-1 after launch customer Eastern, flew on February 9, 1963. Certification of the 727-100, as it was now called, was achieved by December 24 the same year. Eastern flew the first scheduled 727 service on February 1, 1964. In its second year of service, disaster struck as five 727s crashed within months of each other. All crashed on final approach after suffering a rapid rate of descent. The Federal Aviation Administration (FAA) and NASA investigated the 727 and dis-covered that pilots needed to stick religiously to the flight manual to prevent excessive sink rates. The aircraft was cleared and sales continued at between 80 and 100 a year.

With extra capabilities already in mind, Boeing announced the -100C cargo version in late 1964. This was fitted with a large cargo door in the forward fuselage, a strengthened floor, and a cargo handling system. It could also carry some passengers and could be converted into a combined cargo/passenger carrier within two hours. A later model, designated -100QC, allowed conversions to be made in just 30 minutes.

Even as the -100 was entering service, it became obvious that a stretched version would offer increased range, payload, and revenue. The -200, announced in 1965, was a -100 that was stretched by 20 feet, enabling it to carry up to 189 passengers. Other than the sheer length of the -200, the only discernable difference between the two was the shape of the No. 2 or tailfin-mounted engine intake.

By the early 1970s, the 727-100 line was rapidly winding down as the longer -200 prospered. As airlines turned to the bigger -200, various other large companies began looking on the -100 as one of the ultimate corporate jets. This -100 was delivered to the ITT Corporation in November 1971, just 11 months before Boeing handed over the last of 572 short-bodied trijets. Other users of this big biz jet have included W R Grace and Company, and the Saudi Arabian government.

The 727-200 became popular not only with the major U. S. carriers, but also with several European flag-carriers. The national Spanish airline, Iberia, joined Lufthansa, Air France, TAP of Portugal, and Alitalia in the European 727 club. This particular 727 first flew on February 2, 1973, and was delivered to Iberia 12 days later.

Sporting the colors of Laker (the comeback airline owned by Sir Freddie Laker who pioneered discount trans-Atlantic travel with DC-10s in the 1970s) this 727 taxies at Fort Lauderdale, Florida, on a hot March afternoon.

The -100 had an oval shape, but on the very first flight it was discovered that irregularities in the flow of air caused the jet to surge. This phenomenon, which was the jet engine version of a burp or belch, was cured by placing small projections called vortex generators in the lining of the S-duct that led the air down to the engine in the tail. This helped regulate the airflow in the duct as it was sucked down to the engine. The -200 featured a perfectly round intake with the same dimensions as the inlets on the outboard engines.

Later versions of the 727-200 benefited from higher thrust versions of the JT8D engines. The -200

Advanced, with JT8D-17s, was able to fly 1,845 miles (2,970km) with a 40,000 pound payload and full fuel reserves. By the late 1980s, these final variants of the 727 helped make the trijet the best-selling jetliner in history, an achievement that was to be eclipsed only by its smaller sister, the 737.

Quiet Time

Boeing 727s face four major enemies as they soldier on into the mid-1990s: increasing age, a three-crew cockpit versus the standard two-crew cockpits on modern types, strict noise regulations, and more efficient replacements.

The sharply swept wings and triple-slotted trailing edge flaps of the 727 are well picked out by the twilight as this
30

Mexican-registered -200 series launches into the evening sky over Las Vegas, Nevada.

An Air Jamaica 727-2JO provides a bright splash of color to Miami International Airport, Florida, as it nears the end of a flight from Kingston. This represents one of the ultimate development models of the -200, the Advanced, with more powerful versions of the Pratt & Whitney JT8D engine and ramp weights up to 210,000 pounds, compared to only 160,000 pounds for the earliest production -100s.

Captured on camera in the twilight of its career with Eastern, this 727-225 swings toward the departure runway at Atlanta's Hartsfield International Airport in April 1990. Following the collapse of Eastern, this trijet was converted to a freighter and operated by Arrow Air.

Upgrade programs have been devised to keep the 727s in the air. To allow the aircraft to continue operating at night, the upgrades have focused on reducing engine noise. The most comprehensive modernization has been performed on 727-100 freighters flown by the United Parcel Service. The UPS fleet is being re-engined with the Rolls-Royce Tay 651 turbofan, which easily meets the more stringent Stage 3 international noise laws. The aircraft are also being upgraded with digital "glass" cockpits to replace the standard electro-mechanical cockpit displays.

Other fleets, such as that flown by FedEx, are being "hushkitted." Hushkitting involves the addition of engine modification kits that were developed by an engineering branch of FedEx working in close conjunction with Pratt & Whitney. The resulting modified engines are much quieter than the originals. Other more ambitious projects include the possible replacement of the three JT8Ds with just two modern V2500 turbofans made by International Aero Engines. Although the modernization would undoubtedly keep the 727 flying well into the 21st century, it is not yet known if sufficient market interest exists to make such a progam worthwhile.

No matter what the retrofit market does, the sheer number of 727s still flying means that this Boeing workhorse will continue to be found earning a living around the world for at least the first decade of the next century.

Despite its increasing age, the 727 design retains a sleekness that is rare in more recent types. The slim fuselage and compact wing of a Continental Airlines 727-243 Advanced are shown to good effect in this picture taken on the ramp at Phoenix Sky Harbor International Airport.

First of the many . . . the prototype 727 rests in the hands of Seattle's Museum of Flight after serving United Airlines for 27 years. Realizing the historical significance of the 727, United Airlines donated the venerable trijet to the museum in January 1991 after it had flown 64,492 hours, completed 48,057 cycles (one takeoff and landing per cycle) and carried more than three million passengers. The aircraft, first flown in February 1963, is pictured at the museum restoration site at Paine Field, Everett in 1995.

CHAPTER THREE

737

A Baby Called
Fat Albert

The story of Boeing's "baby" airliner, the twin-jet 737, represents the most remarkable turn-around of any jetliner ever built. For the first few years of its life, the little airliner struggled along with so few orders that at one point, it was almost canceled! Who would have thought it would later bounce back to become the best-selling jetliner in history.

In 1964, Boeing faced a major decision. Should it stick solely to development of larger aircraft, like a stretched 707 to combat the DC-8-60 series being developed by Douglas; or should it join the fight for the short-haul market and build a small jetliner to compete with the DC-9 and the British Aircraft Corporation (BAC) One-Eleven?

The small aircraft market was too tempting to resist, despite the fact that Boeing was coming late to the party. Toward the end of 1964, the first DC-9 was nearing completion in California and already had attracted around 200 orders, while the BAC

USAir was launch customer for the stretched and re-engined 737-300 family. One of the airline's early -300 models inherited with the purchase of Piedmont in 1989 is pictured on short finals at Phoenix Sky Harbor International Airport. Also well illustrated in this view are the triple-slotted flaps that give the 737 family its good short-field performance.

One-Eleven was in flight test in the UK and had scooped big orders from giant U. S. airlines like American. Seemingly betting against the odds, the Boeing board gave a tentative go-ahead for the 737 in November 1964.

The early 737 design studies were very different from the jetliner that took to the air in 1967. The aircraft was originally envisioned as a smaller 727 without the third engine. The two jet engines were to be tucked close to the rear of the fuselage beneath a T-tail, resembling both the DC-9 and One-Eleven. The aircraft was also designed to take a maximum of 85 passengers and use the same thrust reversers, starters, and forward nacelles as the 727.

After wind tunnel studies, Boeing engineers predicted that putting the engines beneath the wing would produce marginally less drag. The extra weight of the hanging engine also helped hold the wing "down" against the upward forces caused by lift. This provided bending relief which enabled the wing to be made structurally lighter. By freeing up the space around the rear of the fuselage, Boeing was able to move the horizontal stabilizer down from the top of the fin to mount it in the fuselage, making it easier to maintain pitch stability.

The underslung engines, short fuselage, and requirement for short field operations pointed toward a more conservative sweep angle of the wing. The fail-safe, two-spar wing was therefore swept back at 25 degrees, compared to the sharper and more graceful 32-degree sweep of the 727's wing. Another change, one designed to save weight and complexity, was to leave off gear doors so the wheels were exposed in the undercarriage bay when stowed. Wind tunnel tests proved the

The progenitor of more than 3,000 successors, this particular 737 was the first one to be delivered to an airline and only the second off the Renton production line. Twenty-five years after being delivered to launch customer Lufthansa, it was one of almost 1,000 jets placed in desert storage when this picture was taken in April 1994. The prototype 737 is used as a research aircraft by NASA. Only 30 of these short-bodied 96 passenger, -100 versions were made before production moved on to the 6 foot (1.8 m) longer -200 series.

36

A 737 on lease to America West comes in for another landing in 1990. Each time a jetliner takes off for another flight, or cycle, its fuselage is pumped with pressurized air to maintain a breathable atmosphere in the cabin. This constant pressurization and de-pressurization is particularly wearing on hard-working short-range airliners like the 737, which often fly two or three times as many cycles as their long distance counterparts. This early 737-222, a former United Airlines machine dating from 1969, was last reported lying withdrawn from use and without engines in Arizona.

drag effect was neglible, but it remains unique among jet airliners.

Although the new aircraft began to diverge from the 727 design, it retained 60 percent parts commonality with its larger brother. Much of this came from the critical decision to use the same six-abreast fuselage cross-section as the 707 and 727. The "family" concept first seen in the 707 and 727 was to prove its worth time and time again. The "wide" cabin, combined with the relatively short fuselage, meant that the 737's length (at 93 feet 8 inches) was just 8 inches greater than the wingspan. This effectively created an unusually "square" jetliner.

The German national airline, Lufthansa, was keen to buy the aircraft if Boeing would extend its capacity to 100-seats to compete with the DC-9. Boeing agreed and Lufthansa breathed life into the little airliner program by ordering 22, allowing the 737-100 to be formally launched on February 19, 1965.

United Airlines was Boeing's next major sales victory over the DC-9. United was a loyal Douglas operator and was considering buying DC-9s as part of a larger deal involving stretch DC-8s when Boeing miraculously clinched the 737 sale. Boeing agreed to tailor a slightly longer version of the 737 to United's needs as well as lease the airline 25 727s for an unbeatable rate.

In April 1965, United ordered 40 of the stretched aircraft, now called the 737-200. It was 6 feet longer than the -100 and used a slightly more powerful version of the Pratt & Whitney JT8D-1

The global appeal of Boeing's short-haul jet means that it can be seen in virtually every part of the world. Here a 737-

253 operated by Dragonair coasts in over Kowloon on finals to its base at Hong Kong's Kai Tak airport.

Noise is the main enemy of the older generation 737-200s. Oklahoma-based Nordam is one company which has developed a hushkit, or muffler, for the aircraft's two low bypass-ratio Pratt & Whitney JT8D engines. The kit works by entraining and mixing more air with the core exhaust as it exits the engine.

turbofan fitted to the first aircraft. Later versions of the -200 were fitted with progressively higher thrust versions of the engine, like the 15,500-pound thrust JT8D-15A. This allowed the maximum take-off weight to grow from around 85,000 pounds at the start of the -100 design, to 117,000 pounds for later production models. Ultimate versions of the -200, the advanced high gross weight structure model, were powered by JT8D-15As or 16,000 pound thrust -17As to give a maximum takeoff weight of 124,500 pounds.

The first 737 flew on April 9, 1967, followed a month later by the first production -100 for Lufthansa. Almost immediately the flight test program began showing some ominous shortcomings in landing performance, mostly due to the thrust reverser design. Modified target-type thrust reverser buckets in place of the original cascade thrust reverser design helped solve this problem under a $24 million redesign. Landing performance was also brought back toward original goals with improvements to the triple-slotted flaps.

Other modifications, such as the sealing of gaps in the wing and flaps, helped reduce the drag coefficient, which had been higher than expected, leading to deficiencies in fuel burn and range performance. Modification kits, including the new thrust reversers, were provided as a retrofit for the first 134 aircraft while later production models were fitted with the new features as standard.

Production was also a headache in the early days, as many of the workers on the 737 were relatively inexperienced. The company also realized that production commonality with the 727 was not as complete as was hoped. This was mainly because the smaller jet flew more short hops than its bigger brother, and therefore, it required slightly thicker skins to cope with the higher number of pressurization cycles. In addition, the first wing set failed under a structural test at less than 100 percent of the design load. This meant the production wing had to be strengthened, further adding weight.

Overall, however, the aircraft's performance slowly began to improve and, after a few trying early years, the small jetliner proved itself a money earner. Boeing's confidence in the 737 grew and several special variants of the -200 family were produced to widen its market appeal. The Advanced

The 737 has enabled U. S.-based Southwest Airlines to remain consistently profitable, even throughout the early 1990s, when recession hit the industry and forced several of its competitors into loss and even bankruptcy. By mid-1995 it operated more than 200 737s exclusively. This included 50 older generation -200 Advanced, 125 -300s, and 26 -500s. Incredibly, it also had orders and options for more than 200 additional 737s, most of which were for the first of the new generation 737-700s which is expected to enter service in late 1997.

Boeing 737s are spearheading the inexorable spread of western jetliners into the countries of the former Eastern Bloc. A 737-500 on lease from Ansett Worldwide Aviation Services to Balkan Bulgarian is pictured on approach to at Moscow's Sheremetyevo with a flight in 1994 that only the year before was the domain of the Tupolev Tu-134.

737-200 became the standard production model and by the time production ended in mid-1988, some 1,114 had been delivered. This includes 19 T-43A navigational trainer versions for the U. S. Air Force. Another military variant, the Surveiller, was produced for the Indonesian Air Force, which uses it for maritime surveillance and as a general government transport.

A popular version is the -200C/QC, a convertible passenger/cargo aircraft with a 7 foot 1/2 inch x 11 foot 2 inch (2.15 m x 3.4 m) cargo door, a beefed-up fuselage and floor structure. Some 104 were built by Boeing during the -200 series production run and several more passenger versions have since been converted to freighters by specialist companies.

The Second Generation

The 737 gained a new lease on life with a new type of engine that was developed in the late 1970s by General Electric and Snecma (France). The CFM56 was a high bypass ratio turbofan which produced more power than the JT8D but with far less noise and better fuel economy.

At the same time, the world's noise legislators were beginning to define new operating limits for

aircraft. It was clear that the CFM56 would help keep the 737 alive and popular well into the future. In short, it was the right engine at the right time.

Boeing's biggest problem was how to put the new engine in the same location as the original slimline powerplant. The distinguishing feature of a high bypass ratio engine is the large diameter fan which, in the case of the 737, measured 52 inches. Working closely with the engine makers, Boeing devised a new nacelle with a flattened base to keep it clear of the ground. To the suprise of many, the peculiar looking intake actually proved to have better aerodynamic qualities than the original.

The CFM56-3B was also mounted farther forward of the wing on a new pylon and suspended higher off the ground. The nacelle was also fitted with a distinctive fence on either side which helped keep the airflow smooth over the wing surface above and behind, particularly when the aircraft was at a high angle of attack, such as takeoff and climb out.

Using the CFM56 as the starting point, Boeing began work on the 737-300 in 1980. It lengthened the fuselage by 8 feet 8 inches (2.64 m) by inserting a 3 foot 8 inch (1.12 m) plug forward of the wing

The CFM56 engine made the 737 into a "good neighbor." In the United States, this is most important at John Wayne Airport, in Orange County where airlines are permitted to operate only Stage 3 compliant jetliners. Here an Alaska Airlines 737-400, the longest version of the family until the

arrival of the -800 in early 1998, makes a spirited departure as it launches into a steep climb on maximum takeoff power. Less than a minute later, thrust will be drastically reduced as it coasts out over Newport Beach before climb power is restored and a course laid in for Seattle.

Winter sunshine cleanly lights up the leading edge devices on the stubby wing of this British Airways 737-200 as it climbs out of London Heathrow on a cold January day.

42

and a 5 foot (1.52 m) plug behind the center, or carry-through, part of the wing. The longer fuselage allowed the new 737 to seat up to 149, compared with a maximum of 130 in the -200, as well as providing extra space for an additional 193 cubic feet (5.47 m sq) of freight in the lower hold.

The wing was also strengthened to take the additional loads of the heavier aircraft and its bigger powerplants. The full-span leading edge slats outboard of the engine were modified, as were the trailing edge flap sections, tracks, and fairings behind the engine area. The wings were extended at the tips by 11 inches (0.28 m) and an extra set of spoilers were added. The tailplane span was also increased and a larger dorsal fin added to help longitudinal control in the case of an engine failure.

Production go-ahead was given in March 1981 with orders being placed by carriers like USAir and Southwest Airlines. The first 737-300 took to the air on February 24, 1984, and deliveries started to

USAir in November that year. The first revenue service was actually flown by Southwest on December 7, 1984.

The higher thrust of the CFM56 suddenly gave Boeing a lot more options with the basic 737 and it took advantage by announcing an even larger version, the -400, in June 1986. The new variant was stretched again, this time by 10 feet (3.05 m), with a 6 foot (1.83 m) plug forward of the wing and a 4 foot (1.22 m) section aft. Total length was increased to 119 feet 7 inches (36.45 m) overall, making it just 13 feet shorter than the original 727.

The first -400 flew in February 1988 and was delivered to Piedmont Airlines the following September. Later that year, Boeing developed a high gross weight variant of the -400 with increased fuel capacity, and a strengthened overwing fuselage structure.

By now the looming potential of a replacement market for the original -200 family was becoming

A 737-200 of Nicaraguan operator NICA climbs out of Miami, Florida. Soon, its gear and flaps will retract in prepartion for a fuel-efficient cruise.

apparent. Boeing decided that the best replacement for the first 737 was a new 737 and began development of a 1000-variant using the new technology of the -300 and -400 series as a platform. The company decided to return to the number sequence of the family tree and launched the new variant as the 737-500 in May 1987.

The new 737-500 was shortened to 101 feet 9 inches (31.01 m), making it just over one foot longer than the original -200. The first -500 flew on June 20, 1989, and after a very short (375 hour) flight test program, the first production model was handed over to its launch customer, Southwest Airlines, in February 1990. A year later, Boeing delivered the 2,000th 737, a -500 to Lufthansa, the original launch customer of the 737.

The Next Generation

In June 1987, the 737 became the world's best-selling commercial jetliner when orders reached 1,831, surpassing the previous record held by the 727. However, even with orders later reaching beyond the magic 2,500 barrier, Boeing saw that something more was needed to protect its small and midrange market for the future.

Boeing was driven by several factors, one of which was stiff competition from the European-built Airbus Industrie A320. Much to Boeing's

The constant inspection and upkeep of high-cycle airframes is a never-ending requirement. Here a Malaysia Airlines

737-200 is prepared for maintenance in one of the airline's hangars at Kuala Lumpur.

44

The flattened base of the CFM56 engine nacelle is well illus-trated on this 737-429 of Belgian flag-carrier Sabena as it comes into land. The curious shape of the intake was devel-oped to ensure adequate clearance between the engine and the ground and ended up actually producing a slight improvement in engine performance!

dismay United Airlines, launch customer for the -200 series way back in 1965, chose the A320 over the latest 737 models on offer. Boeing's old rival, McDonnell Douglas, was also busy developing the MD-90—a drastically modified MD-80 with highly efficient and environmentally friendly V2500 turbofans made by International Aero Engines. In addition, Douglas was also beginning to study the MD-95, a 100-seater DC-9 replacement powered by the advanced BMW Rolls-Royce BR715 turbofan. Boeing was also aware of demand for a 727 replacement from loyal customers who wanted to use a Boeing for nonstop transcontinental flights. The 757, launched into the market in 1982, was largely aimed at the 727 operators, but instead carved out a new niche of its own.

Boeing also wanted to look after its huge customer base established with the 727, and later the 737. All this demanded a new and flexible product.

After gathering customer ideas and requirements for two years, Boeing began to define the Next Generation 737-X program. Most of the operators it talked to wanted to keep the things that endeared them to the 737, such as its reliability and simplicity, but needed longer range, slightly higher cruise speed, and lower operating and maintanance costs. Boeing realized that it needed a radically revised wing and an advanced engine to meet the requirements and compete effectively with the competition.

The resulting 737-X family was offered in three major models, a 737-300X, -400X, and -500X. Each

A busy evening at Phoenix Sky Harbor International Airport where the bulk of America West's operations are conducted with both new and not-so-new generations of the

737. The airline runs one of the original -100s as a specially configured 86-seater for the Phoenix Suns professional basketball team.

would have a different fuselage length to provide a range of passenger capacities from 108 seats in the -500X to 184 seats in the -400X. To ensure a family fit for the 757, Boeing decided to offer a stretched version of the original -400. While all three models shared the same newly increased wingspan, the short-bodied -500X was only 102 feet 6 inches (31.2 m) long, the -300X at 110 feet 4 inches (33.6 m), and the -400X an impressive 129 feet 6 inches (39.5 m) long.

The larger span wing was designed with increased chord to improve aerodynamic efficiency at higher speeds and altitudes. This answered customer requirements for 0.79 to 0.82 Mach cruise speeds and a 41,000 foot altitude capability. The bigger wing, with 25 percent more area overall,

also held over 30 percent more fuel to give all the new models a 3,000 nm transcontinental range, almost 1,000 nm more than most of the earlier models. New airfoil technology also meant that the 1960s vintage triple-slotted flap of the original design could be replaced with a simpler, double-slotted flap that would still generate the same amount of lift. A simpler leading-edge slat was also developed for the family.

A new version of the CFM56, the -7, was also adopted. In common with the overall performance targets set by Boeing for the 737-X, CFM International designed the engine to have 15 percent lower maintenance costs. The new engine was also made to develop similar thrust levels to the existing

The squat image of the small Boeing twinjet is pronounced in this shot of a USAir 737-300 as it leads the line-up for takeoff on a busy afternoon at Los Angeles International.

generation CFM56-3C series, but burn 8 percent less fuel and produce less pollutants.

Boeing also designed new flexible interior configurations for the family, based on cabin developments made for the 777. The cockpit was updated with several features, including an integrated global positioning system (GPS) and flight management computer.

First to be formally launched was the 737-300X, which became the -700 when loyal 737 operator Southwest ordered it in late 1993. By mid-1994, Boeing was also able to launch the -400X stretch, which became known as the 737-800. Finally, in March 1995, Boeing clinched a significant victory over Douglas when Scandanavian Airline Systems (SAS) ordered the short bodied 737-500X which became the 737-600.

The 737 Next Generation plan involved a rapid succession of roll-outs, first flights, certification efforts, and deliveries. The first -700s, followed quickly by the -800s, and later by the -600s, was rolled of the Renton production line in December 1996. Southwest took delivery of the first New Generation 737 in October 1997. Deliveries of the -800 were expected to begin in early 1998 pending the successful completion of the certification effort. The sales potential of the New Generation aircraft began to show very early in the program. With sales exceeding 500, they set a marketing record for jetliners that, at the time, had yet to fly.

The extended 119 foot 7 inch (36.45 m) length of the -400 is apparent in this view of a British Airways aircraft as it taxies for takeoff at London Gatwick.

The next generation -800 will be 10 feet (3.05 m) longer, making it almost a third longer than the original -200 series.

48

United Airlines drove the design of the -200 in the mid-1960s and stayed with the current generation of the type, *which, 30 years later, now forms the backbone of its "Shuttle by United" network.*

CHAPTER FOUR

747

Queen of the Skies

In the early 1960s Boeing and Douglas battled for the long haul jet market with progressively bigger and better versions of the 707 and DC-8, respectively. But in 1965, Douglas gained the initiative by announcing the "Super Sixty" series of stretched DC-8s. Ultimate versions would have a 4,500-mile range (7,240 km) with capacity for 259 passengers.

Boeing had stretched the 707 as far as the jetliner's compact undercarriage could practically allow and any further variants would have needed a drastic redesign. The case for something new was becoming more compelling with every year. Jet airliners had triggered an unprecedented boom in international air travel. By the mid-1960s, traffic was growing at the astonishing annual rate of 15 percent.

By early 1965, the need for bigger aircraft was being felt particularly at Pan Am. Early talks between Pan Am and Boeing on the options for stretching the 707 led to the formation of a

Pan American's Boeing 747-121 Clipper Juan Trippe lines up for takeoff from London Heathrow. This notable aircraft, registered N747PA, is the second production 747 and was initially called Clipper America when it first flew in April 1969. It was renamed in 1981 in honor of the Pan Am president who launched the 747—the first widebody jetliner—with an order for 25 in 1966.

preliminary design group at Boeing in August that year. So, in December 1965, when Pan Am issued a letter of intent for an aircraft capable of carrying 400 passengers over 5,000 miles, Boeing was already prepared to embark on a new design of awesome proportions.

A new airplane program was in place by early 1966 and in March that year the board gave the project authorization. Although the sheer size of such an aircraft was daunting, the fledgling Boeing program was helped in at least one direction. The enormous engines needed for such a monster were already being developed by General Electric and Pratt & Whitney for the U. S. Air Force's CX-HLS (C-5A) military airlifter competition.

Among more than 50 proposed configurations, Boeing came up with the then radical concept of a "wide-body" airliner with more than one aisle. This idea was completely new, so Boeing was faced with a wide choice of cross-sections and could even choose the number of decks. Ironically, the configuration was guided by the widely held assumption that a new breed of supersonic airliners would eventually displace the big, but slow aircraft as a preferred passenger choice. They predicted the big jet would end up mostly carrying cargo, so its cross-section was designed to accommodate two rows of 8-foot-by-8-foot seagoing freight containers on the main deck, with room for more freight in the belly hold.

This Continental Airlines 747-143 began its career with Italian flag-carrier Alitalia in 1970, who operated it for a decade. None of the other former users of this hard- *working giant exist today, but they included Hawaiian Express, Flying Tigers, and People Express.*

As well as dictating the fuselage diameter, cargo also influenced the basic shape of the airliner, including the distinctive hump which makes the 747 so instantly recognizable. Early designs included all-passenger, full length double- and triple-deckers, but airlines that reviewed the proposals were worried about emergency exits for passengers on the upper levels.

The multi-deck idea for passengers would have died there except Pan Am requested that the design be adapted so that the nose could ultimately hinge upward to provide easy on-off loading of the cargo. As a result, the cockpit was raised up one level to allow for straight-in cargo loading. Boeing designed an aerodynamic fairing to smooth the cockpit lump into the top of the 747. The large fairing behind the flight deck was earmarked for a crew rest area and air-conditioning system housing. Instead, Pan Am suggested using the space for seating and suddenly the double-deck passenger layout was a reality again. The first upper deck arrangements seated eight in most airline configurations. Later stretched upper-deck variants house an extra 69 passengers!

Happy with the deck configuration, Pan Am placed a $520 million order for 25 747-100s in April 1966, which at the time was the most valuable order ever placed. The program was formally launched in June 1966 as Boeing scrambled to

The sheer size of the 747 is well illustrated in this busy night scene at Singapore's Changi International Airport. Boeing 747s from Qantas and Air India have just arrived while the KLM 747-206B is prepared for its long return flight to Ams- *terdam. This aircraft later worked for Virgin Atlantic and Garuda before going into desert storage in the United States. In 1995, it was flown to Israel for conversion into a 534-seater for use by French carrier, Corsair.*

complete an entirely new factory adjoining Paine Field in which to create the massive jetliner.

The new Everett site, 30 miles (48 km) north of Seattle, had already been selected as a place to build the new C-5A freighter for the U. S. Air Force, should Boeing's design win. In the event Lockheed won the C-5A competition with the Galaxy, so the $200 million Everett facility became solely the domain of the 747.

The construction of the new factory was as awesome as the new aircraft project. A vast tract of dense forest was cleared to build the assembly site, including a huge factory which covered 43 acres under one roof. This remains the largest volume industrial building in the world, especially since it was extend-ed for the 767 and 777 assembly lines. Hills also had to be flattened and valleys filled in. In fact, more earth was moved than was used to build the Grand Coulee Dam.

Boeing began assembling the first 747 from more than 800,000 parts sent to Everett from sub-contractors and other Boeing factories while the factory was being finished around them. The assembly workers progressed at a feverish rate, anxiously attempting to meet the rather ambitious roll-out date of September 30, 1968—less than three years after Pan Am's letter of intent and slightly more than two years after program launch.

As it came together, observers saw that, other than its sheer size, the design of the 747 itself was

Taxiing in to the gate at Moscow's Sheremetyevo after its long trans-Siberian flight from Seoul, is a Korean Air 747SP-B5. To enable it to fly up to 7,650 miles (12,320 km) with 276 passengers, Boeing exchanged weight for fuel capacity by shortening the whole aircraft by 47 feet 1 inch (14.3 m). The tip of the tail was also raised by an extra 5 feet (1.5 m) to handle performance changes caused by the shorter body.

evolutionary rather than revolutionary. Structurally and aerodynamically it bore a strong resemblance to the 707. Tail and wing surfaces were made from aluminum alloy covering dual-path, fail-safe structures. The huge fuselage was made traditionally using frames and stringers covered with stressed aluminum skin. Some more advanced technology bonding techniques were used, but fabrication was essentially similar to tried and tested methods used on the 707, 727, and 737.

The wing was swept back to 37 degrees. This turned out to be a compromise between Boeing's engineers, who had an early preference for the 707's 35 degrees, and Pan Am, who wanted a high-Mach capable wing swept around 40 degrees. The compromise angle turned out to have excellent high-speed cruise qualities, and the 747 continues to fly faster than any commercial transport except the supersonic Concorde.

The same wing also supported a comprehensive array of low-speed devices which allowed the 747 to use 707-length runways. The huge triple-slotted trailing edge flaps were cleverly packed away into the wing for cruise. When deployed, they combined with leading edge flaps outboard and Krueger flaps inboard to produce impressively slow speeds for takeoffs and landings.

Another dramatic new feature was the 16-wheel main undercarriage. Built to withstand the massive stress of landing a 600,000-pound aircraft

In 1980, Boeing announced the availability of the 747-300, which differed from previous models in having a stretched upper deck. By extending the upper forward fuselage aft by 23 feet 4 inches (7.1 m), top deck accommodation was boosted from 32 to 69 passengers in an all-economy configuration. Swissair, which took delivery of the first -300 in March 1983, later started to operate Combi versions of the -300 like the aircraft pictured here at Zurich.

at speeds of 150 mph, the main gear had four hydraulically retractable four-wheel bogies. Two were mounted side-by-side under the fuselage (level with the trailing edge of the wing) and retracted forward into the belly. The other two bogies helped spread the load on runways and taxiways and were mounted under the wing root area. They were set slightly forward of the other pair and retracted inward toward the fuselage. The nose gear was a conventional two-wheel unit that retracted forward.

By going to a big, complex four-gear arrangement, Boeing was able to use standard, 707-size wheels. It was also safer, as landings could still be made if even half the tires were blown. A 747-400 proved this by landing safely at Los Angeles Inter-national with hydraulic failure with only two of the five undercarriage legs down!

The high bypass ratio engines that made the entire development possible also gave Boeing a few headaches in the first few years of the 747 program. Pratt & Whitney had developed the JT9D turbofan in competition with General Electric for the C-5A. Although the GE TF39 won the U. S. Air Force work, the Pratt engine found a good home on the 747 after major modifications for its commercial role. A later civil derivative of the GE engine, the CF6, also powered later 747s.

The initial JT9D generated up to 39,000 pounds of thrust, more than double the highest powered version of the JT8D on the 707. However, the first 747 had put on too much weight during its devel-

The explosion of passenger traffic in Asia is directly tied to the 747, and particularly the latest - 400 version where more than half of the present fleet is used. Here a Japan Air Lines 747-446 passes the crowded Kai Tak ramp on short finals for the runway projecting into Hong Kong Harbor. Of the first 1,000 747s made, more than 400 were based in Asia. Europe and North America each had around 250 with the balance being shared between the Middle East, Africa, and South America.

opment and now weighed in at close to 710,000 pounds, against the original design estimate of a little over 600,000 pounds. This made it a harder task for the JT9Ds, which could not take the early 747s to their planned maximum altitude of 45,000 feet.

In addition to being underpowered, the first JT9Ds were very unreliable. Pratt & Whitney was, in a way, pushing the technological envelope harder than Boeing. It was dealing with technical issues and demands that no other engine manufacturer had encountered in the commercial world. The manufacturer had to devise new solutions to strange problems not usually encountered on lower bypass engines. The huge engine casings, for example, would turn slightly oval in shape because the engines supports were too flexible. This caused turbine and compressor blades to rub against the walls, which destroyed the delicate tolerances and drastically affected performance by reducing pressure ratio and cycle efficiency. The large front fan also made the big engine difficult to start in crosswinds.

Engine problems dogged the 747 certification program, which involved the prototype, RA001 (N7470), and four production series aircraft. Some 55 engine changes were made during 15 months of flight tests. Even up to two months before certification in December 1969, problems got so bad that at one point in October, some 22 brand new 747s were parked at Everett waiting for serviceable engines. In the end, Pratt & Whitney overcame the seemingly unending string of technical nightmares

The 747 is truly a world-shrinker. No version, nor operator, is a better reflection of this than the 747-438s flown by Australian national airline, Qantas. Dubbed by the airline "Longreach," each of the Rolls-Royce RB211-524G-pow-ered aircraft carries 400 passengers with bags for almost 8,300 miles (13,350 km). This Qantas "Longreach" is pictured on finals at Heathrow, seconds away from the end of its long flight from Australia to England.

to make the JT9D one of the most successful turbofans. Some 17 major versions of the engine were eventually developed, later resulting in high-performance engines such as the JT9D-7R4H1, with a whopping 56,000 pounds of thrust.

Even training pilots to taxi the giant aircraft demanded new techniques. To simulate the sensation of being in a flightdeck 29 feet above the ground, equal to a three-story building, a 747 cabin was mounted on a tower placed in a truck. The training crew simulated taxiing by using a radio to instruct the truck driver when to turn.

The 747 made its maiden flight on February 9, 1969, just under two months later than its planned target date of December 17, 1968. The flight was a

success, though a flap problem forced the test crew to conduct the entire mission with flaps in the deployed position. The aircraft was found to handle with the responsiveness of a much smaller aircraft, delighting pilots who had feared it would be slow and cumbersome.

Later test flights, however, unearthed a flutter problem at high speed. This was traced to interaction between the aircraft's huge, but relatively thin 5,500 square foot (511 sq m) wing, and the 8,470-pound weight of the underslung engines. It was corrected by adding weights to the front of the outboard engine nacelles. In later production aircraft, flutter was eliminated altogether through the use of a heavier wing structure.

Only the distorted view through a fish-eye camera lens can hope to capture most of the switches, knobs, dials, instruments, and other systems visible in the complex looking cockpit of this KLM 747-200 as it cruises over the North Atlantic from Amsterdam to New York. System integration,

flight deck modernization, and TV-type "glass cockpit" displays introduced on the later 400 series have enabled a switch to a two-crew cockpit with only 365 lights, switches, and gauges compared to over 960 in this flight deck. (See -400 cockpit, p.61)

Commercial Service and New Generations

The first 747, Pan Am's Clipper Young America, entered service on January 22, 1970, traveling from New York to London. Despite being seven hours late due to problems with doors, cargo loading, and engines, the flight was nonetheless a milestone in the history of air transportation, being the first of the wide-bodied airliners that would carry the jet revolution another stage forward.

By late 1970, the early engines were already being superseded by more powerful and dependable versions. The succession of new JT9Ds, and later General Electric CF6 and Rolls-Royce RB.211 powerplants, allowed Boeing to develop an entire family of 747s, each with slightly better performance than the last.

Sales of the original 747-100 were boosted by engine improvements and eventually totaled 167. A revised version, the -100B, was developed with a strengthened wing, fuselage, and undercarriage. Iran Air ordered the first of these powered with the 48,000 pound thrust JT9D-7F in 1978. Production of all -100 versions totalled 205.

In 1973, Boeing delivered the first SR, or short range, version of the -100B. This was developed for the Japanese market where the 550-seater is used on short domestic flights.

The availability of the 45,600-pound thrust JT9D-7A allowed Boeing to develop the longer range

The impressive bulk of a 747-400 is seen as this Air Canada aircraft shows off its new livery. Maximum takeoff weights of 875,000 pounds (393,750 kg), or around 400 tons, are routinely used in -400 operations. Max takeoff weight for the -100, by comparison, is around 710,000 pounds (322,100 kg). The difference between the two is roughly equivalent to the maximum takeoff weight of a fully loaded 737-400!

747-200. The first of these was delivered to KLM Royal Dutch Airlines in 1971. This -200 was the first Boeing airliner to serve with this loyal Douglas operator. More powerful JT9D-7Fs, rated at 48,000 pounds thrust, further boosted performance on later -200Bs.

In the midst of the development of the first few major derivative models from 1969 to 1971, severe financial hardships hit Boeing. This was largely due to a worldwide economic recession but was compounded by huge expenditures on the Everett site, the $1 billion plus 747 development program, and cost overruns on the 737. Despite the cost hurdle of supplemental type certification with new powerplants, Boeing believed the 747 would have wider market penetration with a choice of engines.

As a result, the 52,500 pound thrust General Electric CF6-50E2 turbofan was offered on the -200B, to be followed some years later by the Rolls-Royce RB.211-524. The GE-powered version of the 747-200 was ultimately selected by the U. S. Air Force for the Presidential Transport to replace the venerable VC-137, the military designation for the 707-320. All three engine choices were made available for the -200C Convertible, which, as its name suggested, was convertible from all-passenger to all-cargo, or five combinations of both. The first

A Japan Air Lines 747-246F loads cargo through the side door during a busy evening on the Los Angeles International cargo ramp. The -400 freighter version carries 122 tons, or some 44,000 pounds (19,960 ka) more than the -200. As

well as producing brand new freighters, Boeing also converts passenger 747s into freighters at its factory in Wichita, Kansas. By mid-1995, the factory had converted more than 60 747s to freighters since the first modification in 1972.

-200C was delivered to World Airways in April 1973 with the impressive maximum takeoff weight capability of 833,000 pounds.

All the 747-100 and -200 versions used the same basic structure and it was not until the advent of the -200F Freighter that major changes were made. These consisted of a nose-hinged cargo door to handle straight-in loading and a large side cargo door on the main deck. The 200F was capable of carrying 200,000 pounds of main deck cargo over 4,500 nautical miles (8,340 km). Production of all -200 derivatives eventually totaled 393 69 of which were -200Fs and 223 standard passenger -200Bs.

Another significant model, and one which required major redesign, was the 747SP, or special performance. The SP was designed for long-range routes which could not sustain fully loaded 747s. Although early plans for the aircraft had already been drawn up, Pan Am was again a major focus for the development effort in 1973 when it was seriously considering buying the McDonnell Douglas DC-10.

Boeing toyed with the idea of a three-engined version of the 747 for the SP, including T-tail designs. In recognition of the simplicity, reduced cost, and overwhelming logic of simply shortening the 747 fuselage, it opted to develop the 747SB- or short body. By 1975, when the prototype first flew, it was known as the SP.

Components in the final 747SP design were 90 percent common with the 747 with the major change being a reduction in overall length of 47 feet 1 inch (14.35 m). The wing was also structurally lighter and fairings over the wing-body join were modified to adapt to changing airflow patterns caused by the shortened fuselage. New single-slotted variable pivot flaps replaced the standard 747 units and the tailplane span was increased by 10 feet (3.05 m) to ensure the same stability in pitch as the longer versions. To compensate for the reduced lateral stability potential inherent in shorter body designs, Boeing also increased the height of the tail by 5 feet (1.5 m) and double-hinged the rudder.

The SP was capable of carrying a normal load of around 276 passengers over long ranges of 6,650 nautical miles (12,300 km) at altitudes of up to 45,000 feet. Despite only 45 -SPs being built, most remained in service through the mid-1990s and still command high resale value. Overall sales were disappointing for Boeing and some company cynics suggest the 747SP shows the company is far better off stretching aircraft, and not shrinking them.

The next major structural change occurred in 1980 when Boeing announced the 747-300, which featured a stretched upper deck. The upper forward fuselage was extended aft by 23 feet 4 inches (7.1 m) to provide extra space, and the spiral stairway was replaced with a straight stairway. The new stairway used up less main deck space and provided room for an extra seven seats. First

Sophisticated simulators are now the training norm for crews who operate the 747-400 and its advanced flight deck. This view of a Thai Airways simulator clearly shows the major elements of the integrated display system including the two centrally mounted engine indication and crew alerting system (EICAS) displays. Outboard, the bright blue/green displays are primary flight displays which show speed, altitude, heading, and attitude. The two circular-type images are stylized compass roses on the navigation display. The 400 crew has a workload similar to those of twinjets.

customer for the -300 was Swissair, followed by the French airline, UTA. Deliveries began in 1983.

In 1985, Boeing committed to a major update of the 747 to inject new life into the big widebody. Boeing felt both internal and external pressure to modernize the 747. Internally, the high-technology 757 and 767 programs were well into production and the electro-mechanical 747 was obviously inconsistent with these next-generation airliners.

Externally, airlines were pushing for changes. Many were operating mixed fleets with aircraft built by Airbus Industrie, a prolific advocate of high-technology use in airliners. Additionally, McDonnell Douglas was canvassing carriers with the two-man "glass-cockpit" MD-11, a major derivative of the DC-10.

Not to be left behind, Boeing announced the design go-ahead of their new generation 747, the -400 in July 1985 and first flew it in April 1988. Although externally similar to the -300, the -400 wingspan was increased by 12 feet (3.6 m) and sported prominently swept winglets which cant out by 22 degrees at the tip. Structurally the -400 used many advanced materials to save weight. Advanced aluminum alloys, for example, save up to 6,000 pounds (2,700 kg) in the wingbox area. Composite was used for winglets, main deck floor panels, cabin fittings, and in the engine nacelles.

No matter how good simulators become, there is always a place for hands-on flight training. Here a Northwest
62

747-451 pulls up steeply from a runway in Arizona during crew training before its service entry.

Most of the big changes, and the ones that caused the most problems for Boeing, were made to the avionics and systems. The flight engineer's position was eliminated by a radical cockpit instrument redesign. A six-screen electronic flight instrument system (EFIS) was developed at the core of the effort to reduce the number of lights, switches, and gauges on the flightdeck by around 600.

In efforts to please every customer with tailor-made changes to avionics and internal cabin configurations, Boeing ended up attempting to simultaneously develop versions powered by three different engine types. They underestimated the enormous task and the timetable slipped as a result.

With time and tremendous effort, the -400 program gathered speed and orders. The avionics finally began performing as expected and the aircraft quickly became the lead flagship for most international carriers. By mid-1996, -400 sales accounted for around half of all the 747s ordered since the launch of the program.

Variants included the -400 Combi, a combined passenger/freight aircraft that could carry either 266 passengers and 60,000 pounds (27,200 kg) of freight on the main deck, or up to 413 passengers without the freight. A high-density 568-passenger version called the -400 Domestic was also developed for Japanese carriers.

All the improvements of the -400 were also

Japanese carriers like All Nippon Airways use specially developed high-capacity 747-400s on short routes within the country. The 747-400D (D for domestic) is the only version of the -400 series without winglets, as they are only of real benefit on longer haul operations. This aircraft, seen displaying its vast triple-slotted flaps to good effect, was pictured at Everett prior to delivery in the summer of 1995.

A brand new Cathay Pacific 747-400F freighter takes to the runway prior to its delivery flight to the airline's Hong Kong base. The -400F blends the stronger wing of the -400 series with the original fuselage of the -200 freighter. Externally, therefore, only the winglets distinguish this as one of the heavyweight champions capable of carrying 244,000 pounds (110,670 kg) of cargo. Boeing expects the world cargo industry to grow by more than 6 percent every year through the first decade of the next century, and predicts that nearly 600 more large-capacity freighters (more than 50 tons) will be needed by the year 2014. The -400F first flew in 1993.

combined with the fuselage of the -200F to form the -400F Freighter.

Future Generations

Concerned airlines began asking manufacturers to study aircraft bigger than the 747-400 as the air traffic system began showing serious signs of congestion in the early 1990s. Airbus concentrated on the A3XX ultra-high capacity aircraft (UHCA), an all-new twin deck design while McDonnell Douglas studied the similar-looking MD-12, a four-engined double-decker which was a radical departure from its familiar trijets.

Boeing also began its own studies of a New Large Airplane (NLA), but faced a dilemma. As the only maker with an existing product in the arena, the 747, should it use the 1960s design as the foundation for something new or go for a clean-sheet NLA? A further complication arose out of exploratory talks that Boeing held with the four major airframe partners making up the Airbus consortium. The talks focused on a possible partnership over a project dubbed the Very Large Commercial Transport (VLCT).

By late 1995 two sets of factors forced Boeing back to major derivatives of the 747 which it called the -500X and -600X. First, the VLCT analysis predicted a smaller than expected market of only around 1,000 aircraft. Boeing argued that this was too small a market to warrant partnering on an all-new airplane with an estimated development price tag of around $16 billion.

Second, Boeing's own NLA studies indicated a preference by airline operators for commonality with existing fleets. In other words, a 747 derivative. However, earlier studies had shown that none of the airlines would be satisfied with a simple stretch. The fuselage could be made longer but the 747 wing simply would not support the necessary range or payload. Boeing therefore came up with a blueprint for two highly capable versions—both based around the same new wing. Both aircraft would be developed in parallel to meet varying demands for higher capacity and longer range. By developing two versions, Boeing believed it would be able to meet the immediate call for much larger capacity transports as well as hold onto its top-of-the-range market dominance by producing a perfect successor to the 747-400.

The new wing, a roughly 30 percent scaled up version of the advanced 777 airfoil, was a giant leap beyond the original 1960s aerodynamics of the basic 747 wing. It enabled Boeing to aim realistically at the two main project drivers: noise and performance. By mid-1996 plans were being finalized for the launch of the two variants in quick succession. The 500X was defined as a 465-passenger jumbo with a range of 8,700nm, some 1,400nm greater than the -400. The even larger -600X, with an overall length of 278ft, would seat 550 and still fly 600nm further than the -400. However, hopes of a 1996 launch suddenly faded as airlines studied the competing A3XX and Boeing reconsidered the market size and huge development costs, estimated at around $7 billion. Finally, in early 1997, it placed the whole 747X project on ice to concentrate on further development of the 767-400ERX and 777 twins. The impact of twinjets, and the phenomenon of "fragmentation" of long-range trunk routes, appeared to have put major growth plans for the 747 firmly on hold for the near future at least.

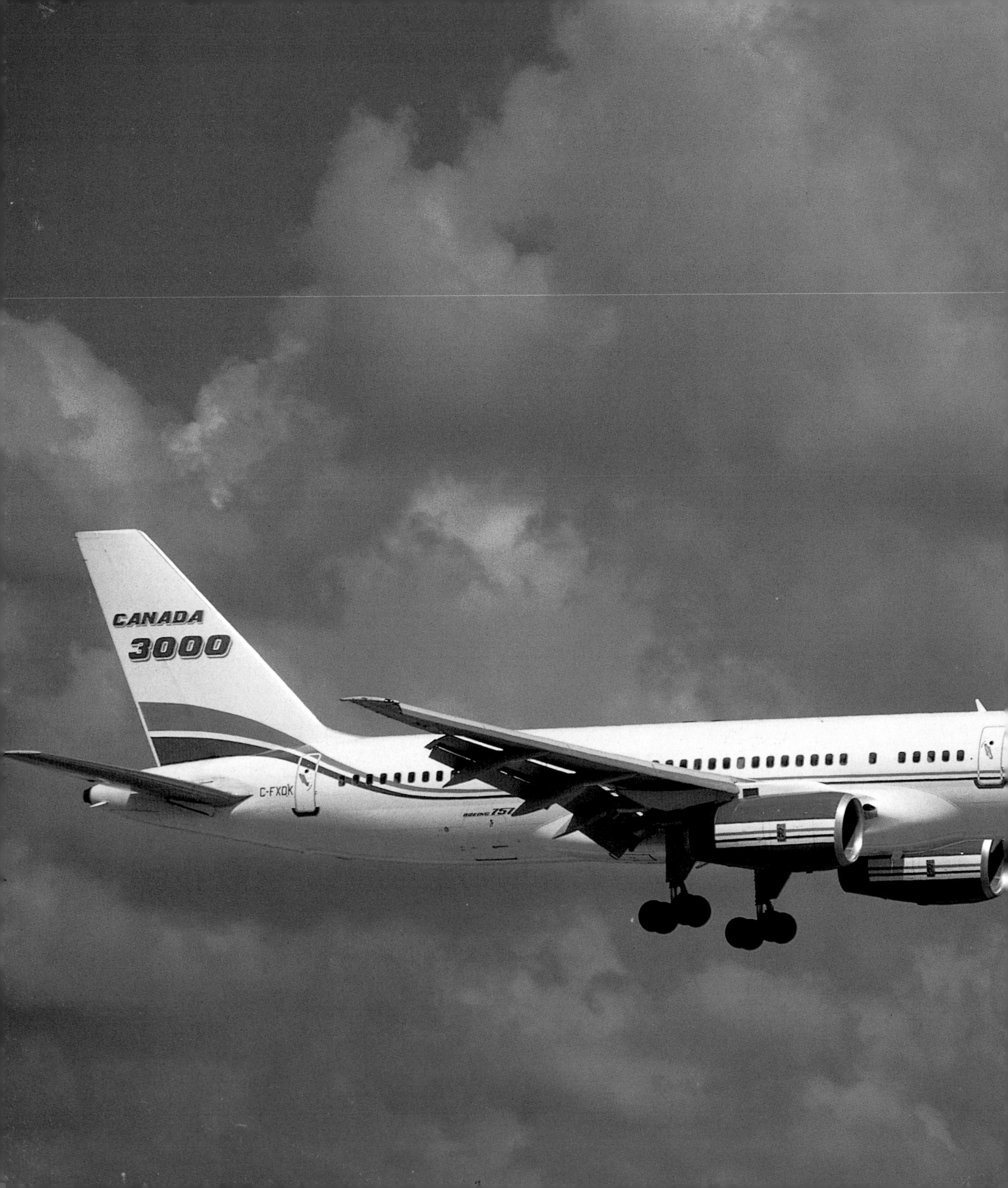
CANADA
3000
C-FXOK

CHAPTER FIVE

757

Big Fan
Narrow-Body

Boeing's spritely 757, although intimately twinned with the 767 wide-body development, began life as a straight-forward 727 replacement.

Boeing began its inevitable search for a 727 successor by examining a large derivative of the trijet as a cheaper alternative to an all-new design. Working with United Airlines, it produced the concept of a stretched 727-300. The longer T-tail airliner was stretched by 20 feet to more than 170 feet in length and had 35 more seats than the 727-200. Improved leading-edge devices and engines maintained the good field performance of the basic 727. The longer aircraft also had larger undercarriage legs.

While the 727-300 program seemed a good prospect, a separate "clean sheet" design also under study offered the potential for far greater operating efficiency. The Arab oil embargo of 1973 and 1974 coincided with Boeing's deliberations on

The flexibility of the 757 allows it to be equally profitable on short shuttle-type networks or on long-range charter flights. Engine reliability has been so good that both Rolls-Royce and Pratt & Whitney powered versions are now cleared for flights across oceanic distances up to 180 minutes single-engine flying time away from diversionary airfields. One such operator is Canadian charter airline, Canada 3000.

The new technology 757 was the first Boeing jetliner to be launched with a non-U. S. engine, when Eastern Airlines and British Airways ordered Rolls-Royce RB211-535-powered versions in August 1978. The fifth production 757, pictured here taking off from Miami, still wore a hybrid Boeing 757/Eastern color scheme when this scene was captured in 1990, shortly before the demise of the airline. This aircraft was flying for Airtours International in the UK by 1995.

the future direction of new designs. Fuel prices soared and the emphasis immediately shifted to more efficient designs.

At the time, Boeing was working on several new materials and aerodynamic design technologies and saw an opportunity to combine them with the second generation of fuel-efficient, high-bypass ratio turbofans. Boeing confidently worked out that aerodynamic improvements could produce 10 percent fuel savings over older designs, while the new engines would provide another 20 percent on top of that.

The new design that eventually emerged suprised many in the industry because it was a narrow-body. At the time, the accepted vogue since the 747 was for new wide bodies, and to some the narrow airliner seemed like a step backwards. However, the company's own research had pointed toward a narrow-body design. It even worked out that passengers preferred narrow-bodied aircraft for short flights. Furthermore, keeping the six-abreast fuselage section of the 727 could mean a 7 percent fuel savings over a seven-abreast section.

Studies also indicated that about 70 percent of all air travel at the time was made up of flights less than two hours long. Given that most short haul travelers want a flexible schedule, Boeing assumed

that an airline would cater to this by flying frequent trips with a narrow-body aircraft rather than a few trips with a wide-body one. Adding all the clues together, Boeing came up with a size that fell into the 727 category, between 160 and 180 seats.

Boeing consequently offered airlines two basic versions of what was dubbed the 7N7—a 160 seat -100 and a 180-seat -200. In August 1978, the two launch customers, Eastern Airlines and British Airways, both ordered the -200 version of what had by now become the 757. The 160-seater did not attract much interest so the smaller version was never built.

Other plans changed too. As late as 1979, a year after program go-ahead, the 757 design still had a T-tail and used the forward fuselage of the 727. Although the T-tail offered fuel efficiency through lower drag, it was scrubbed because of the better stall recovery characteristics of a conventional tail. The fuselage retained the same dimensions as the 727, but the decision was made to give the 757 a common "glass cockpit" with its big new brother, the 767.

This was a clever idea that had already been tested, to a much lesser degree, with the electromechanical 747 and 747SP cockpits. Although the 757 and 767 are completely different in weight and size, the common-cockpit concept made sense because the two aircraft were being developed almost at the same time. Common instrumentation would be cheaper to procure and certify. It would also make things cheaper for the airlines too. If airlines bought both, then crews would get common type ratings. This vastly cut training costs, simplified crew scheduling, and allowed a common seniority roster.

Boeing managed to use the same cockpit in both types by an ingenious geometric compromise. In the narrower 757, the flight deck was a step down from the cabin floor level, while in the 767, the flightdeck was reached with a step up. In addition to the actual instrument display and general cockpit layout, the two front windows were also common.

Other common parts included the air conditioners, auxiliary power units, hydraulic system parts, and the electrical power system. Above all, the 757 and 767 shared similar configurations overall, which made development easier and created similar flying characteristics.

One such feature was the 757's graceful 124 foot 10 inch (38.05 m) wingspan, which used virtually the same aerofoil cross-section as the 767. It

British Airways has used its 757 fleet mainly on "Super Shuttle" and major European trunk routes since it was first introduced into UK service in February 1983. Here a 180-seat version approaches Heathrow completing its evening flight from Glasgow.

The 757s high power-to-weight ratio gives it an excellent takeoff and climbout capability. Here a Rolls-Royce-powered

757 operated by Columbian airline Avianca soars into the afternoon sky over Miami.

The 757 has proven to be a popular sized aircraft for many new operators, including start-up airline Transaero of Russia. This 190-seater was newly delivered to the

fledgling operator when it was photographed at Terminal One of Moscow's Sheremetyevo airport before a flight to Norilsk, Siberia.

was swept at 25 degrees, the same as the 737 wing. This was significantly less than the 767's 31.5-degree wing sweep. The lower sweep was acceptable because of the 757's lower average speed. Although both aircraft cruised at Mach 0.80, the short- to medium-haul 757 spent a lot of each flight climbing and descending.

The advanced wing design was one of the first "aft loaded" sections used in a Boeing jetliner. It had a relatively flat top and a slight inverse camber underneath the trailing edge. This gave the same effect as a supercritical wing, which generates lift right across the upper surface instead of concentrating it close behind the leading edge. This also meant that drag rise at higher Mach numbers was delayed. The relative stiffness of the wing also allowed Boeing to use all-speed, fully powered ailerons outboard, with no requirement for inboard ailerons.

The engines hung from the wing in traditional Boeing style and, as usual, provided structural bending moment relief by weighing down the wing against the lift forces. This allowed the wing structure to be kept relatively light. Precise use of the fuel tanks in the wing also helped this process, but only if used in a certain order. Engineers therefore designed the engines to first use up fuel in a huge center tank that extended outboard almost as far as the engines.

One of the most impressive features of the 757 was its set of sophisticated high-lift devices, including double-slotted flaps and full-span slats. The flaps operated by track and carriage to give the aircraft an excellent short-field capability. Air and ground braking was assisted by five spoilers on each wing with one additional spoiler per wing for ground use only.

With the steep hills behind Kowloon for a backdrop, China Southern 757-200 B-2818 taxies out in preparation for the short flight from Hong Kong to Guangzhou. By the mid-1990s, the dependability and power of the 757 was such that aircraft operated by another Chinese carrier, China Southwest, were cleared to begin regular flights into Bangda airfield at 14,219 feet (4,334 m) in the Tibetan Himalayas. This is equivalent to flying from the top of Mount Whitney in California, the highest point in the contiguous United States. The one hour air service from Bangda to Chengdu in Sichuan province saves a journey that can take up to five days by road.

Boeing's program goal was to produce a new aircraft that could achieve 40 percent more seat-miles per gallon of fuel than the 727. To achieve this it made unprecedented use of composites and advanced aluminum alloys. It aimed to save about 2,000 pounds on each 757, for a fuel savings of around 30,000 gallons per year. In the final product, Boeing virtually doubled its design performance goals.

Carbon fiber reinforced plastics (CFRP) were used to make the rudder, ailerons, spoilers, and engine cowls. Kevlar-reinforced plastic was similarly used for access panels, pylon fairings, and fin and tailplane tips. A hybrid mixture of CFRP and Kevlar was used for the undercarriage doors, wing/fuselage fairings, and flap track fairings. Altogether the composites were used for a weight savings of almost 1,500 pounds. A further 610

pounds were saved by using advanced aluminums. Boeing also shaved another 1,500 pounds of weight off the 757 as it was being developed through a weight-reduction program.

In parallel with the 767 program, the 757 also expanded the amount of major subassembly work that was subcontracted out to other companies. In the case of the 757 around half the aircraft was made by Boeing itself.

One of the avionics milestones achieved by the 757 was the use of the all-new Engine-Indication and Crew Alerting System (EICAS). It consisted of a pair of CRT displays made by Rockwell Collins that replaced the normal engine instruments. Its purpose was to continually scan the aircraft systems for abnormalities, flashing up any findings. Although the 767 flew five months before the 757, the EICAS display was not fitted in the 767 until the fifth aircraft.

An Air Canada 767-200 comes into land as two 757-200PFs (package freighters) operated by Miami-based Challenge Air Cargo stand ready to take new loads with their large 134-inch-by-86-inch (3.4-m-by-2.18-m) cargo doors hinged upwards. Most of the 757-200PFs produced are flown by overnight freight specialist, United Parcel Service.

The first few flights of the 757 were therefore the first flights of the EICAS. It proved its usefulness on the maiden flight of the prototype, N757A, on February 19, 1982. The first aircraft was powered by Rolls-Royce RB.211-535Cs, a 37,400-pound thrust version of the original RB.211 series developed for the Lockheed L-1011 Tristar. Pratt & Whitney was developing the PW2037 and the more powerful PW2040, but neither would fly soon enough, so the 757 became the first Boeing jetliner to be launched with a non-U. S. engine.

During the flight, the EICAS indicated a problem with one of the engines well before it would have shown up on conventional instruments. During a test designed to investigate handling qualities with the No. 2 engine cut back to flight idle, the engine stalled.

The crew wanted to restart the powerplant using a windmill-start. This utilized forward airspeed to assist the relight in a process similar to push-starting a car. However, the EICAS warned the crew that the oil pressure was too low in the No. 2 engine to attempt a windmill-start, meaning that they would have to go through a longer air-start procedure. But the crew was reluctant to shut the engine completely down if it did not have to, so they began the process for a windmill-start by advancing the throttle. The fuel flow increased slightly, as did the exhaust gas temperature, but the rpm did not increase.

The crew then performed a normal air start. The incident had proven a vital point: the EICAS was doing precisely what it was designed for and had confirmed that the engine was outside the windmill-start envelope. This helped increase crew confidence in an untried system.

Double-slotted trailing edge flaps, full-span leading edge slats, and a new aft-loaded wing section provide the 757 with excellent low-speed handling and landing characteristics. An Aero Peru 757-200, leased to the carrier by Ansett Worldwide Aviation Services, is pictured here touching down at Miami on an afternoon service from Lima.

The distinctive polished aluminum skin of two American
Airlines 757-200s stands out against the gray concrete
of the Miami ramp. American is gradually growing its
757 fleet toward 100 aircraft as older 727-100/200s
are phased out. The airline's weight-saving habit of pol-
ishing instead of painting its aircraft is likely to continue
as it strives to save costs. It has worked out that if its
260-strong McDonnell Douglas MD-80 fleet was paint-
ed, for example, it would cost roughly $365,000 per
year in extra fuel.

On the second flight, the EICAS again flashed up a warning when the 757 lost a hydraulic system after landing. It indicated that there was a loss of hydraulic fluid in the system. A conventional warning system would not have even marked the event until the hydraulic system was almost completely spent.

The new sophistication of the EICAS was matched by the other elements of the new-look flight deck. Along with the 767, the 757 was the first commercial application of laser gyros which formed part of the Honeywell inertial reference system (IRS).

In the IRS, a computer detects minute differences in the time taken for laser light to travel between mirrors inside the gyro. The difference is converted into a calculation of movement which the IRS passes to the flight deck TV displays in the form of position, velocity, and attitude information.

Some sophisticated avionics, including laser-based (rather than mechanical) gyroscopes, were introduced for the first time commercially on the 757 and its larger twin counterpart, the 767. This 757, operated by MGM Grand Air, is pictured sitting in Las Vegas.

A Honeywell flight management computer system (FMCS), fed with air data from another computer, provides automatic en-route and terminal area navigation. It also works out the most efficient route by calculating both vertical and lateral flight profiles. The FMCS is linked to automatic-flight-control and thrust-management systems to ensure that the flight profiles can be followed precisely.

The 757 was certified by the FAA on December 21, 1982, and entered service with Eastern on January 1, 1983. The twin was certified by the UK CAA (Civil Aviation Authority) on January 14, 1983, and began service with British Airways the following month. The first Pratt-powered aircraft entered service with Delta Air Lines just over one year later.

Boeing discovered that the 757 market appeal was far wider than either the 727 replacement role or the 500-mile design range it had worked to. Airlines opened up entirely new market niches with the aircraft, which, in some ways, began to complement rather than directly replace the 727-200. Other airlines, particularly European-based charter operators, also started to use it on long-range routes. Eventually the aircraft's excellent safety record allowed it to be cleared for extended range twin operations (ETOPS).

The aircraft's payload, range, and exceptionally low noise levels became attractive to United Parcel Service (UPS), motivating them to ask Boeing to develop a 757-200PF (Package Freighter) version. The -200PF has a large freight door cut in the forward side and can take up to 15 standard 88 x 125 inch (2.2 x 3.2 m) cargo pallets on the main deck. A mixed passenger/freight Combi version was also developed and is used by Royal Nepal Airlines.

In late 1995, Boeing announced studies of two new 757 derivatives. One of them, the long anticipated 757-300X stretch, was expected to become a firm program. The other, a long range -200X derivative, was offered to airlines interested in using the 757 to open up "thin" international routes that could not support larger aircraft.

The -300X version was aimed at expanding the large niche that the 757 had carved for itself in the charter business, particularly in Europe.

The long legs of a 757 reach for the runway as it nears touchdown on an evening flight. High lift systems and advanced aerodynamics allow approach speeds as low as

132 knots (245 km/h) at max landing weight, and even slower at normal landing weights.

Boeing planned the simplest possible stretch program by inserting two plugs forward and aft in the fuselage. Overall length was increased by around 23 feet (7m) while passenger capacity was boosted by 20 percent from 198 to 235 in a typical configuration.

The stretch got the go-ahead at the 1996 Farnborough air show when German carrier Condor ordered 12. Major assembly began in 1997 and deliveries were due to start in 1999, making it the shortest design to delivery of any Boeing derivative program. The new initiative was designed to stimulate further life into the 757 which, by early 1997, had amassed 870 orders.

Every type of Boeing jetliner has eventually been offered in a freighter configuration and the 757 is no exception. United Parcel Service launched the 757PF (package freighter) with an order for 50 in 1990 and was still receiving new models in 1996. Behind this UPS 757, receiving last-minute attention before delivery, stands an ex-Eastern Airlines 757 undergoing conversion into a research platform for NASA's Langley Research Center.

CHAPTER SIX

767

Widebody Twin

Boeing claims the 767 has done more for the cause of wide-bodied twin jets on extra long range routes than any other product. Throughout the 1990s it has come to dominate the North Atlantic, the busiest longhaul route in the world. Furthermore, it achieved this in head-to-head competition with the Airbus A310 and A300-600R.

Like so many other Boeing products, it's eventual role evolved radically away from the original intent. The early 1970s saw the spread of wide-bodies on short, medium, and long-haul routes around the world. The Airbus A300, Lockheed L-1011, McDonnell Douglas DC-10, and Boeing's own 747 completed the assembly. Boeing saw an opportunity to open a market niche with a new wide-body, smaller than the DC-10 and L-1011, in the trans-continental market.

Due to the long-range potential of the 767, Boeing soon developed heavier weight versions with a fuel tank in the center section to enable it to tackle routes up to around 6,180 miles (9,950 km) and more. Scandinavian Airline Systems (SAS) was keen to exploit the long-range capabilities of the big jet on its trans-Atlantic and Polar routes. This SAS Pratt & Whitney PW4056-powered 767-283ER is seen on short finals to London Heathrow. By 1995, some 33 carriers regularly operated the 767 across the North and mid-Atlantic.

With thrust reverser just stowed, and leading edge slats and trailing edge flaps still deployed, a Britannia Airways 767-204 slows to walking pace at Bristol Airport, UK, at the end of a charter flight from mainland Europe. With seating for 290, and the range and performance to operate from regional airports directly to most of the popular inclusive tour destinations, the 767 has become a useful moneymaker for the UK's biggest charter carrier.

As was the case with the 757, which actually lagged slightly behind the 767 in development timescale, the signs were right for a new, more efficient product. The high fuel price scare of the 1973–74 Arab oil embargo and the looming prospect of new environmental rules on aircraft noise helped drive the initiative. In addition, a lot of environmentally unfriendly 707s and DC-8s were going to need replacing on domestic trunk routes by the early 1980s. Boeing was determined to keep competition from Airbus at bay.

The 7X7 program duly began to shape, and by 1976 was evolving into a twin-aisle design with three engines and a T-tail. In the end, only the twin-aisle feature survived, the trijet arrangement losing out to the twin in the battle for fuel economy. The T-tail option was held until fairly late in the design but, like the 757, later succumbed to the superior stall-recovery characteristics of a conventional tail.

Boeing was still pulled in different directions on the number of engines by two potentially huge customers, American and United. American, which had formed an affection for its DC-10 fleet, still preferred a trijet. United wanted just two. Eventually Boeing decided that it had better offer two versions, a twinjet 7X7 with onestop transcontinental range and a trijet version with nonstop transcontinental range.

Not happy with the obvious compromise, Boeing completed a rigorous design study of the two versions and concluded that the twin, with seats for about 180 to 200 passengers, was by far the better bet. The case for the twin was compelling—fuel costs had by now become so high that they formed almost half of an airline's direct operating costs.

Ironically, another reason for discarding the third engine was the fact that there was no long-range over-water requirement, so an enormous amount of weight and complexity was saved by only having two engines. Who could have guessed that the new plane would become a leading pioneer of transoceanic twin operations?

In February 1978, Boeing got board approval to begin offering the new plane under its new name, the 767. Not suprisingly, United became the launch customer with an order for 30 in July

Like nearly every Boeing before it, the big twinjet was ripe for stretching. In 1983, Boeing began work on the 767-300, which was given a 10 foot 1 inch (3.07 m) plug forward of the wing and an 11 foot (3.3 m) plug behind the wing. Delta Air Lines, which followed United in ordering the 767, was also interested in the -300 and eventually ordered the longer range -300ER version. One of the Delta fleet is shown here climbing out of Los Angeles International on a summer day.

American Airline's long haul moneymaker is the 767. Happy with its -200ER fleet, one of which is seen here on finals to land, it placed the launch order for the stretched -300ER in 1985. The -300ER fleet now forms the core of its international network fleet with more than 40 in service. By mid-1995 the 767 was the most numerous twin on long distance routes around the world, with 49 airlines using it for ETOPS (extended range twin operations) services.

that same year. The very next month the narrow-body 757 twin received launch orders and suddenly Boeing found itself simultaneously developing two brand new products.

By the time the 757 formally received a production go-ahead in March 1979, the two programs had become intertwined. To increase development and production efficiency, reduce costs, and boost marketing appeal, the two developments would become practically symbiotic. Both would use common advanced technology cockpit and avionics, advanced materials, basic design features, and limited use of computerized design.

The two-man, all-digital cockpit was devised to counter the ever-increasing pilot workload. The core of the clean, uncluttered flight deck display was formed around six CRT displays, hence the term "glass cockpit." The CRTs could be used to display an infinite variety of data, including complex engine information that normally preoccupied the flight engineer at a dedicated cockpit station.

CRT and avionics technology had reached a critical level of maturity. The units were bright enough to be seen even in direct sunlight and, most important, they were reliable. The CRT became the pilot's main instrument, although a

Maximum seating in the -200 series is up to 290, requiring over-wing exits like those visible on this El Al aircraft. The relatively chubby -200 can also hold up to 22 LD2 or 11 LD1 containers in the underfloor cargo hold. Even more space is available below the main deck of the longer -300. Boeing has also sold dedicated freighter versions of the 767-300 to United Parcel Service and Asiana of South Korea.

back-up set of electromechanical instruments were left on the console as insurance.

The 767 cockpit was given two types of CRT displays—an electronic flight instrument system (EFIS) and an engine instrument and crew alerting system (EICAS). The EFIS displayed an electronic attitude director indicator (ADI) and a horizontal situation indicator (HSI). The HSI was adapted to be used as a map display with track, navigation beacons, and even weather radar information superimposed. Each pilot had four EFIS displays while the center console showed the EICAS on another two displays.

Although the 757 and 767 could share a common cockpit they were worlds apart in fuselage cross-section. Deep consideration over the 767's cross-section led eventually to a seven-abreast arrangement. Although one seat narrower than its closest competitor, the A310, the slightly slimmer fuselage produced less drag, translating into a 2 percent fuel savings. The familiar Boeing double-bubble section, instead of the A310's circular cross-section, was carefully arranged and sculpted to position the floor level at just below the halfway point and give the cabin an almost vertical side wall.

Cabin comfort received more emphasis with the 767 than in any previous design. Careful interior architecture and lighting gave the illusion that the cabin was actually bigger than it was—a

Another holiday charter 767 user is British inclusive tour airline, Air UK Leisure. Here one of its 767-300s displays the wing's track-mounted leading edge slats and double-slotted inboard trailing flaps as it lands at London Gatwick.

trick now used by virtually every manufacturer. A new toilet with a suction drainage system, or "sewer" that ran the length of the cabin (allowing toilets to be located almost anywhere) replaced traditional, but more troublesome, toilet systems. The twin-aisle, seven-seat arrangement also meant that 80 percent of the passengers could use window and aisle seats, rather than the unpopular center seat.

Achieving the performance goals outlined at the beginning of the program demanded the very best from powerplant and aerodynamics. For the first time Boeing launched a new jetliner with a choice of engines, either the General Electric CF6-80A or Pratt & Whitney's JT9D-7R4. Within months a choice was also offered on the 757 and on the 777 a decade later.

The engines were held snug to the wing with a broad pylon to give as much ground clearance as possible and to eliminate the need for an extra large undercarriage. Positioned relatively close inboard to the fuselage, at under a third of the span, the engines were still well clear of most debris that could be thrown up by the nosewheel or thrust reversers. The position also provided best controllability in case of an asymmetric failure.

Aerodynamic improvements contributed to the 30 percent fuel burn savings that were claimed for the 767 over older types. Most improvement came from the wing, which, like the 757, used an aft-loaded aerofoil section with a relatively flat top and inverse camber beneath the trailing edge. This was used because wing thickness could be increased without suffering a much larger drag penalty. The thicker wing carried more fuel and could easily accommodate a complex set of slats and flaps. Some 16,700 gallons (63,200 litres) of fuel could be stored on current -200/300 models. Capacity has since been raised to more than 24,000 gallons for the latest long-range versions.

The 31–30 degree sweep angle of the wing gave a good elliptical distribution of lift over the span of the aerofoil. This reduced the amount of drag encountered at cruise speeds around Mach 0.80. The sweep angle, combined with the 156 foot 1inch (47.6 m) span and just over 28 foot (8.6 m) wing chord, produced some 3,050 square feet (283 sq m) of wing area. Such a large area gave the 767 good high altitude cruise capability and, more important, allowed Boeing to stretch into the -300 model without modifying the basic wing design.

The tailplane, like the wing and tail fin, was a conventionally built two-spar design with stressed skin. Borrowing from the 707 design, the all-moving tailplane had a carry-through center section and was controlled by a single screw-jack. For the first time, Boeing used a single-piece rudder operated by three hydraulic jacks.

Manufacturing improvements also accompanied the 767, including the use of CAD. Even though Boeing had only planned on designing 20 percent using CAD, by the end they used it for nearly 35 to 40 percent. A new kind of rivet with three times the fatigue strength of traditional

The extra 10 foot 1 inch (3.07 m) length of the stretched forward fuselage of the -300 is accentuated in this overhead view of a Gulf Air -300 as it soars out of London Heathrow on an October day at the start of a flight to Bahrain.

84

counter-sunk rivets was also used for the first time on a commercial aircraft. More advanced assembly techniques were also used including a semi-automatic wing spar assembler.

Composites were used extensively in the first 767s for a weight savings of 1,250 pounds. Like the 757, composites like carbon fiber reinforced plastic (CFRP), Kevlar reinforced plastic, and glassfiber-reinforced plastic (GRP) were most prominent. While it was still gaining confidence in this relatively new material, Boeing restricted the use of composites to secondary structures like ailerons, elevators, spoilers, rudder, access panels, engine cowls, undercarriage doors, and wing/ fuselage fairings.

Advanced aluminums were used not only to save weight but also to improve stress resistance. Use of the alloys on the upper wing skin, for exam-

ple, allowed stress levels to be raised by around 10 percent. New alloys were used for a weight savings of around 650 pounds on structures like spar booms, webs, wing stringers, and forgings.

International involvement reached an unprecedented level in the 767, representing to some extent the increasingly linked relationship between national interest and the equipment choice of national airlines. The biggest slice of the action went to Japan, where three manufacturers (Fuji, Kawasaki, and Mitsubishi) made the wing fairings, main landing gear doors, center body fuselage panels, exit hatches, wing in-spar ribs, rear fuselage body panels, stringers, passenger and cargo doors, and the dorsal fin.

Alenia, the Italian aerospace company, also had a large chunk of the program making wing control surfaces, flaps and leading edge slats, wingtips, elevators, fin, rudder, and nose radome.

The distinctive one-piece pods of the Rolls-Royce RB211-524G turbofans help identify this British Airways 767-336. At a thrust rating of 60,600 pounds (270 kN), the RB211 is the most powerful engine option available on the 767, though only British Airways and one Chinese operator had chosen this powerplant by 1997.

Thrust reversers slow down a Qantas 767-300 as it lands at Singapore after a flight from Australia on a hot tropical day. In the foreground a 767-3T7ER operated by EVA is pushed back from the gate to commence its flight to Taiwan. By *mid-1995, Boeing estimated that 767s had carried 546 million passengers on 3.3 million flights since the type first entered service on September 8, 1982.*

North American subcontractors included Vought and Grumman, now both part of Northrop. Between them they made the wing center section and adjacent lower fuselage, lower fuselage bulkheads, and horizontal tail. Bombardier's Canadair of Canada made the rear fuselage while Boeing Helicopters, Philadelphia, manufactured the wing's fixed leading edges.

Construction of the first 767-200 started on July 6, 1979. Two years and two months later, the Pratt-powered aircraft took off on its maiden flight. Other than problems with the center hydraulic system and a faulty toilet flush valve, the flight went well. Later tests at high speeds and altitude indicated that an artificial pitch stability system was not needed if just seven vortex generators were fitted on each wing.

The integration of the sophisticated new avionics presented some problems, but these were eased by the shared responsibility with the 757 development team. Once Boeing eliminated an oversensitivity problem in the digital systems which produced false alarms, it moved on to refining the flight control and thrust management systems. This latter device automatically controlled engine thrust to precise levels dictated to it by the flight management system.

United took delivery of its first 767 in August 1982, and Delta took delivery of the first General Electric-powered aircraft in October that same year. An extended range version, the first 767-200ER was developed and flew in 1984. Tankage was increased by opening up the center fuel tank and optional gross weight was ultimately increased to 387,000 pounds—87,000 pounds more than the basic version.

In 1986, Boeing flew the first stretched -300 version. It had a greater passenger capacity at 269, compared to 220 for the basic model. Although it had the same gross weight as the -200 series, the aircraft was stretched with a 10 foot 1 inch (3.07 m) plug forward of the wing and an 11 foot (3.3 m) plug aft. The longer aircraft was strengthened around the undercarriage, on parts of the fuselage, and on the lower wing to cope with the extra stress.

Having witnessed the beginning of the ETOPS revolution with the -200ER, Boeing pressed on with the -300ER. The -300ER offered a maximum optional gross weight of 400,000 pounds, a full 100,000 pounds beyond the original model! Maximum range for the -300ER was more than 6,000 nm (11,200 km), or almost double the range of the first -200.

Boeing is developing military versions of the -200, including tanker/transports and an airborne warning and control system (AWACS) version. A civil freighter version of the -300ER has also been developed. It can carry a 90,000 pound (40,800 kg) payload over 4,000 nm (7,400 km), or 112,000 pounds (50,800 kg) over 3,000 nm (5,550 km). The major customer for the -300ER is UPS, as they hold orders and options for 60. A general freighter version capable of carrying perishable cargo has also been ordered by Asiana Airlines of South Korea.

Further versions of the 767 under consideration for possible launch in 1997 included the proposed -400ERX version which was stretched by around 21 feet (6m). This offered a 10 to 15 percent increase in seats, 25 percent more lower hold volume, and up to 10 percent cut in seat-mile costs. The -400ERX would have winglets, new landing gear, a maximum range of around 6,500 miles (10,450km), and an increase in gross weight. More than 725 sales booked were by 1997.

Like the freighter version of its smaller sibling, the 757, the cargo-carrying 767-300F was also launched by UPS, who placed orders and options for up to 60. Here, the first production version, N301UP, takes a break between flight tests at Everett.

Long after the certification program was completed, the 767 prototype took on a new life as the Airborne Optical Adjunct for the U. S. Defense Department's Strategic Defense Initiative (SDI). The ungainly cupola sitting atop the fuselage houses infrared tracking cameras that are used to make high-altitude sightings of missiles in midflight. The large ventral fins were added to compensate for the directional instability caused by the cupola. Since the demise of SDI, the 767 is now designated the airborne surveillance testbed and is used for a similar role in other U. S. military programs. Behind it sit two E-3 AWACS (one NATO and the other USAF), a role that will be taken over by the 767 in the future. Farther off sits the 757 prototype, which is used as a research testbed. Note the dark area on the port wing of the 757 used for laminar flow research.

CHAPTER SEVEN

777

The Seventh Wonder

The Boeing 777 is the world's largest twin-engined aircraft and uses the most powerful jet engines ever developed. Amazingly, it is also the first all-new Boeing aircraft since 1978 when the company began designing the 757 and 767.

The 777 is the first aircraft to be designed entirely on computers and is Boeing's first jetliner to employ a digital "fly-by-wire" flight control system. Altogether the 777 uses three times the amount of composites of any previous Boeing aircraft. This is evident in the aircraft's large tail, which is comprised almost entirely of composites.

The seeds for its seventh jetliner were sown in late 1986 when Boeing began studying a potential replacement for large fleets of McDonnell Douglas DC-10s and Lockheed L-1011 Tristars. The 767

From a distance only the sheer, 747-like size of the 777 distinguishes it from the 767. Closer inspection, however, reveals a very different aircraft with a six-wheel bogie on each main undercarriage leg, "gulled" inboard wings, and a sharp blade tailcone. This United Airlines 777-200 is pictured making its first visit to London Heathrow during a whistle-stop world tour in April 1995. A few days after the photograph was taken, this aircraft set a world speed record by flying 7,850 miles from Bangkok to Seattle in 13 hours 36 minutes on June 7, 1995.

89

seemed like the right place to look for a new jet that would fit between the DC-10, 767-300, and 747-400.

The 767-X, as the study was called by December 1989, gradually identified that a whole new design was needed rather than another stretch of the 767. The company's original intent was to satisfy the niche by extending the range and capacity of its existing wide-body twin to about 300 passengers. The study revealed more interest in bigger and bigger aircraft and the 767-X option began to run out of steam. The seven-abreast cross-section meant that a longer stretch would become too long for most airport ramps.

Pressure for something more than a 767 derivative also mounted from the airlines which were being offered a brand new family of airliners by Airbus and a radically updated DC-10 called the MD-11 from McDonnell Douglas. The medium-range Airbus A330, long range A340, and the McDonnell Douglas MD-11 were already beginning to take orders and had already signed up a combined total of 57 operators when Boeing eventually gave the 777 program the firm go-ahead in October 1990.

But to Boeing there was a silver lining to this black cloud. By turning its tail-end position to its advantage, Boeing could look at the competing designs, now fixed and in production, and go one better. It eventually responded to the A340 and MD-11 designs with a bigger cross-section, newer interior, greater flexibility, and larger size, just as Douglas had done 20 years before by designing the DC-8 to be a little larger than the 707.

The final design was still far from clear, however. Some potential customers proposed ideas for a twin-engined jetliner capable of carrying 25 percent more passengers than an L-1011. It would also use the modern flight deck of the 747-400 and seat 10 abreast in economy, or coach class. Others suggested a family of types, like the Airbus approach.

To understand exactly what the airlines would like in this new design it adopted a brave new iniative for an airliner manufacturer, market-driven product development. In the days of the 707, the airlines (the customers) were almost the last people

consulted on the details of a design once the basic principles had been settled. In more recent times, they became involved in the latter stages of avionics and interiors. This time the manufacturer invited the airlines to actually participate in the design from day one.

A "gang of eight" world class carriers were invited to say what they wanted to see built into the "clean sheet" aircraft. In January 1990, technical representatives from All Nippon Airways, American Airlines, British Airways, Cathay Pacific, Delta Air Lines, Japan Air Lines, Qantas and United Airlines began regular "working together" meetings with Boeing.

The working together concept immediately took off and quickly pervaded the entire program. The idea was extended to cross-functonal design build teams (DBTs). DBTs brought together team up of up to 40 customers and suppliers involved in a particular part of the aircraft. At one point, more than 238 different DBTs were active on the 777 working on its various components. The company has been so pleased with the improved efficiency of designing a new aircraft in this way that it remains a model for all future projects.

In the first airline group meeting, each came up with different suggestions in response to a 23-page Boeing questionnaire. One thing they all agreed on was a wider fuselage than either the A340 or the MD-11. As a result, the 777 fuselage is almost 25 inches wider than the A340 and 7 inches (17 cm) wider at elbow level than the MD-11. The cabin therefore provided Boeing with the starting point for the rest of the design, becoming the first airliner to be designed specifically from the inside out. The company chose the moment to opt for a perfectly circular cross-section instead of the "double-bubble" used for every other Boeing jetliner.

Boeing then worked out what to build around the new fuselage. It examined two-, three-, and four-engine arrangements. It even reviewed a bizarre hybrid which mated a 767 fuselage with a small section of 757 fuselage riding on top. The "Hunchback of Mukilteo," as it was named after an area local to Everett, was dismissed because it did not offer enough cargo space and, more important, did not look right!

Comparitive studies showed a four-engined design would be 20 to30 percent higher in cost, while a twin was 10 percent lower. A twin, however, would need the most powerful engines ever developed for an aircraft. Engine makers assured Boeing that powerplant size would not be a problem if it decided to build a twin. The company therefore opted for a two-engine arrangement, avoiding the extra cost of a new four-engine design and the structural issues of a trijet. The fact that no suitable modern engine existed for the four-engine thrust requirement either (about 40,000 pounds), helped Boeing confirm its decision.

The wing design had to meet multiple requirements. It had to be big enough to allow the 777 to grow into a wide range of models, all of which would be heavier than the first versions. It also had to allow the aircraft to cruise at higher speeds than the 767 over longer ranges, yet still fit into gate spaces used by DC-10s to ease fleet compatibility for airlines. To solve this conundrum, Boeing came up with the ingenious notion of designing a folding wing, just like an aircraft carrier-based aircraft. The normal wingspan is 199 feet 11 inches (60.9 m), but with the wingtips folded the span is reduced to 155 feet 3 inches (47.3 m).

With the option of a folding wing as back-up, Boeing was able to design a wing with the optimum span for a quick climb and high cruise capabilities. The result was the most efficient aerofoil section ever used by a Boeing jetliner. It has a 31.6 degree sweepback and high thickness for economical structure. Its large internal volume contains either 31,000 gallons (117,335 litres) of fuel in the first version or 44,700 gallons (169,190 litres) in the heavier takeoff weight version.

By March 1990, the working together groups had produced the basic foundation for what would become an entire family of all-new 777s. The first of the family was to be an "A" market, transcontinental DC-10/L-1011 replacement capable of carrying 375 passengers in two-class seating over a range of 3,970 nm (7,340 km). This would compete directly with the A330 on routes like New York–San Francisco, Denver–Honolulu, London–New York, or even Tokyo–San Francisco.

Further down the line, Boeing planned to beef-up the structure and offer a "B" market intercontinental range aircraft. Externally identical to its "A" market stablemate, the longer range 777 would carry 305 passengers in a tri-class layout on ranges up to 6,300 nm (11,170 km). Later, heavier versions were planned with range capabilities in excess of 7,400 nm (13,700 km). These aircraft would fly in head-to-head competition with the A340 and MD-11 on longer-range routes like London–Los Angeles, Tokyo–Sydney, or Chicago–Seoul.

Using the heavier structure of the "B" market as a foundation, Boeing planned to stretch the 777 to take around 450 passengers in two-class seating over ranges similar to the original "A" market aircraft. The 777-300 would be stretched with two plugs, forward and aft of the wing, to make it 242 feet 4 inches long compared with the original 777 length of 209 feet 1 inch. The stretch also made it a few feet longer than the 747.

The stretch 777 was made possible by the tall and strong main undercarriage design. This big main unit carries a six-wheel bogie making it the most distinctive undercarriage of any Boeing since the 747, and the largest ever used in a commercial aircraft. A six-wheel arrangement was chosen to keep pavement loading down to similar levels as the DC-10-30, but without the need for a center-main post. The stretch was aimed as a long-term replacement for earlier 747-100s and -200s. A stretched "B" market and a super long-range 777-100 market aircraft also featured on the original 777 roadmap.

Happy with the "A" market aircraft it had helped so closely to design, United placed the launch order for 34 firm plus 34 options on 15 October 1990. Two weeks later, the Boeing board of directors gave the formal go-ahead for production and the New Airplane Division—which had been formed to oversee the 767-X development—was renamed the 777 Division of the Boeing Commercial Airplane Group.

The 777 is the first Boeing jetliner to be designed from the cabin outward. Largely as a result of this approach, the 777 is also the first Boeing jetliner to be perfectly circular in section. The BA aircraft are powered by the General Electric GE90, the largest jet engines ever built. The GE90 intake measures 123 inches in diameter—within inches of the fuselage diameter of the 707 and its narrow-body successors.

Design of the aircraft was by now virtually complete. The 777 was the first large commercial airliner to be designed completely on computers using a Dassault/IBM CATIA three-dimensional computer-aided design system. This system allowed Boeing to fit every part together in cyberspace before any real metal had even been cut. The use of digital

more or less perfectly while the port wing tip was out of position by only 0.001 of an inch! These miniscule design variances on a project as large as a 777 were nothing short of a miracle.

The complex new avionics, digital fly-by-wire (FBW) flight control system, and sophisticated cabin entertainment system also demanded bold new iniatives. With the integration nightmares of the 747-400's advanced cockpit still fresh in Boeing's collective memory, the company spent $370 million on an Integrated Aircraft Systems Laboratory (IASL). This was used like a complete "skinless" aircraft to make sure the complex systems worked properly both individually and collectively.

Another vital reason for the IASL was Boeing's commitment to deliver the first 777 ready for instant service in daily airline use, either domestically or over long extended-range twin operation (ETOPS) routes. Most new airliners take months, or even years, to have niggling snags ironed out before they achieve high despatch reliability levels. Boeing's goal, agreed with United, was a 98 percent despatch reliability level from day one in service. Even more ambitious than delivering it "service ready" was the goal of instant ETOPS.

All long-range twin-engined aircraft earn ETOPS certification to operate over long barren oceanic or wilderness routes by flying for thousands of trouble-free hours. This convinces the regulatory authorities that it is statistically safe for the aircraft to fly on routes which are sometimes up to three hours single-engine flying time away from the nearest airport. Boeing and United proposed to earn this ETOPS credit by the time the first 777 was delivered in May 1995. The IASL was used to build up reliability levels to such an extent that a rigorous flight demonstration period immediately before final delivery would gain the necessary approval.

Each of the three different engine types used on the 777 were also required to prove high reliability in advance by running for thousands of hours on ground-based endurance tests. Pratt & Whitney's PW4084, a big engine based on the PW4000 series core but with a large new 112-inch diameter fan, was selected by United, and

pre-assembly was a major achievement of the 777 program and helped cut down change and rework by 65 percent, some 15 percent better than Boeing's goal. When the enormous fuselage sections were put together on the first aircraft, for example, the alignment from nose to tail was out by only 0.023 inch. Similarly, the starboard wing tip was positioned

therefore was first to be used. General Electric, which was developing the brand new, truly enormous, GE90 was next, having suprised the airline world by beating Rolls-Royce to the British Airways order. The GE90's 123 inch inlet diameter was just 16 inches narrower than the fuselage of the 707 prototype. The Rolls-Royce Trent 800, selected by Cathay Pacific and others, was the third to fly.

The IASL was used to integrate and test a complex network of systems that all relied on an electronic highway called the ARINC 629 multiplex digital databus. The sheer sophistication of the 777 and its ambitious ETOPS goals meant that nothing less than the 629 could be used. Eleven of these databus highways connected all the avionics systems together allowing two-way communication at the rate of up to two million bits per second.

Eight major subsystems were tested in the IASL, including the brakes, landing gear, electrical power generating system, leading edge/trailing edge devices, electronic engine controls, and autopilot. It also tested out the aircraft information management system, or AIMS, which were the avionics' "brains" of the 777. The AIMS contained some 600,000 lines of software code. It integrated display, communications, flight and thrust management, data-conversion, engine-data, and flight-data acquisiton all into a single cabinet. The 777 has two AIMS cabinets, each one of which could fly the aircraft alone.

By combining so many functions into the AIMS, Boeing was able to make a 20 percent weight saving, a 30 percent power reduction, and a 100 percent improvement in basic reliability. It also meant that other systems, like satellite communications and GPS navigation (installed on all 777s) were easily connected with the rest of the avionics.

After testing as subsystems, the elements were further integrated into one of three major test sites in the IASL. One of these, the systems integration lab (SIL) checked the function of the 777's electrical, avionics, and sensor systems and made sure they all "talked" to each other. Up to 400 simulated "flights" per month were made by the SIL.

Another major facility within the IASL was a cockpit cabin simulator where the interplay between the autopilot, flight director, AIMS, and other systems took place. The 777 flightdeck used the 747-400 baseline avionics design combined with the twinjet systems design of the 767. Unlike either, however, it introduced the use of six flat panel displays, as opposed to heavier, bulky CRT displays.

The third IASL lab was the flight control test rig which checked the interoperability of hydraulic and mechanical systems with the FBW flight control system. The 777 was Boeing's first FBW aircraft, though the company had gained some experience through military programs and the abortive 7J7 propfan project.

Another new development for the company was the construction of a passenger cabin engineering lab (PCEL). This acted like a mini-IASL but was used just to test the highly complex electronics of the cabin and its entertainment system. Much of the 2.6 million lines of software code developed for the 777 were used in the cabin where a core cabin management system controlled interphones, lights, and temperature control. Inflight entertainment systems for the 777, including seat-back or arm-housed video screens and audio stations, made up more than 2,000 individual units weighing more than 6,000 pounds.

The cabin itself was carefully designed with "zones of flexibility" arranged throughout its length. These were pre-engineered to house wiring, plumbing, and attachment fixtures so that galleys, toilets, and bulkheads could be easily rearranged into different configurations. Large, drop-down overhead compartments were a design innovation to offer large stowage capacity.

An unprecedented amount of advanced structures were also used in the new aircraft. Some 2,600 pounds (1,180 kg) of weight was saved by using composites. Also, for the first time on any Boeing jetliner, composite was used for a primary structure. In this case the torque box of the fin was mostly made from a carbon-fiber reinforced material and only the auxiliary spar was made from aluminum. The rudder was made from carbon-fiber epoxy sandwich panels attached to carbon-fiber spars and ribs.

Composites were also used for moving wing trailing edge surfaces and spoiler panels, wing fixed leading edges, engine nacelles, wing root fairings and main landing gear doors. Some 3,200 pounds (1,450 kg) were eliminated through the use of advanced aluminums.

Roll-Out and Flight Test.

The 1990s will be long remembered in the aviation community for its succession of ever-spectacular roll-out events. Challenged by impressively theatrical unveilings by Airbus in Toulouse, Boeing decided to make the 777 roll-out a dramatic event for thousands of workers, guests, and the media.

A Los Angeles entertainment company stage-managed the event, and it turned out to be radically different from anything Boeing or its competitors had ever done. Instead of one roll-out, there were 15! This allowed 100,000 workers and their families to see the event, which was repeated every half hour for most of the day on April 9, 1994.

Finally, on June 12, 1994, the first 777 took off from Everett into a leaden Washington sky for a 3 hour 48 minute maiden flight. The aircraft reached a maximum altitude of 19,000 feet (5,846 m) and the crew shut down and restarted one of the Pratt & Whitney PW4084 engines, before returning to Everett.

Test flights continued from Boeing Field, Seattle, and built up in range and scope as more aircraft entered the program. To test the systems reliability in extreme climates, aircraft flew north of the Arctic Circle in search of freezing temperatures and south to Arizona and New Mexico for hot desert conditions. An aircraft spent time at Edwards Air Force Base, California, using the long runways there to test slow speed handling and severe brake tests.

In February 1995, the first GE90-powered 777 made a flawless flight from Everett and joined the sister aircraft of the test fleet at Boeing Field. Although slightly later than scheduled, the GE program was backed up by the engine company's own 747 testbed, which made additional parallel flight tests with a GE90 to deal with any new issues before they cropped up on the 777.

By March, the third and final engine type for the 777, the Rolls-Royce Trent 800, was in flight test on the Boeing 747 testbed and was being readied for first flight aboard the Cathay Pacifc 777. Finally, on April 19, 1995, the P&W-powered 777-200 was certified by both the FAA and JAA, becoming the first Boeing jetliner to achieve simultaneous certification on both sides of the Atlantic. In all, Boeing estimated that the total certification flight test effort from June 1994 to March 1996 would involve nine aircraft and cover more than 6,700 flight hours and 4,800 flight cycles, representing the most intensive test effort in civil aviation history.

The first 777 to enter service was handed over to United in mid-May 1995 and began commercial life by operating the London Heathrow to Washington, Dulles International on 7 June.

In December 1995 the first GE90-powered 777 was delivered to British Airways, and at the end of March 1996, Thai Airways International took delivery of the first Rolls-Royce Trent-powered 777. Orders for the new twin quickly rose to 318 by early 1997, some of which were for the stretched -300, which was formally launched at the 1995 Paris Air Show. Delivery of the first "B market" 777, later renamed 777IGW (increased gross weight), took place in late 1996, while deliveries of the -300 were scheduled for 1998 onward. Boeing meanwhile hoped to launch its shortened 777-100X, or super long range -200 variant, in time for entry-into-service by 2000.

As a result of its broad market applications, Boeing expects to be building versions of the 777 well into the first half of the 21st century.

Index